Classic
AMERICAN
CARS

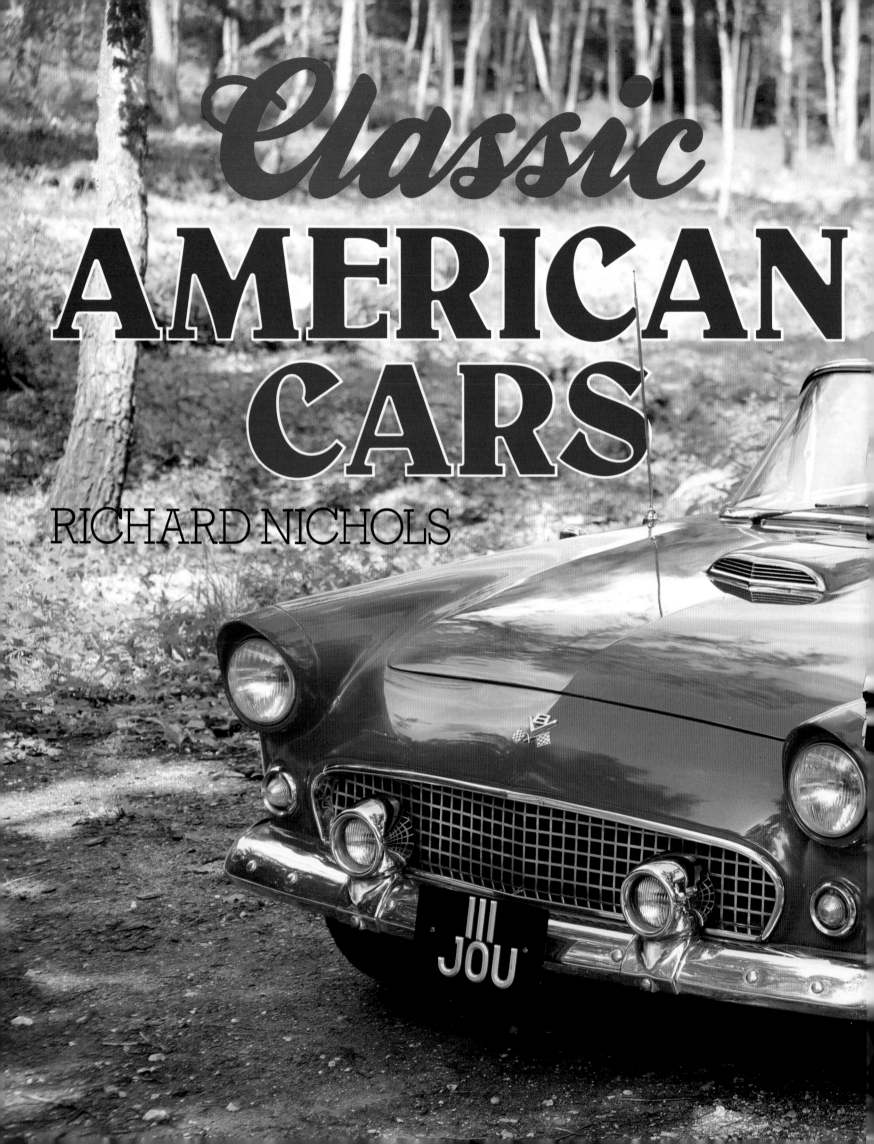

Classic
AMERICAN
CARS

RICHARD NICHOLS

Exeter Books

NEW YORK

🐂 A Bison Book

First published in USA in 1986
by Exeter Books
Distributed by Bookthrift
Exeter is a trademark of Bookthrift Marketing, Inc.
Bookthrift is a registered trademark of Bookthrift Marketing, Inc.
New York, New York.

ISBN 0-671-08193-4

Printed in Hong Kong.

Page 1: One of the most prestigious, desirable and collectable profiles in the business – Clark Gable's 1935 Duesenberg Speedster.
Pages 2-3: The 1955 Ford Thunderbird Convertible – a two-seat 'personal car' which was the Dearborn reply to Corvette, the GM sportscar.
Pages 4-5: 1924 Ford Model T Doctor's Coupe. Henry Ford's Model T was the car which made motoring commonplace and became remarkable because it was produced in such massive numbers.

CONTENTS

1 Model T   6
2 Stutz   12
3 Mercer Raceabout   18
4 Packard   22
5 Auburn Speedster   30
6 Duesenberg SJ   34
7 32 Ford   40
8 Cord 810   44
9 Buick Y-Job   48
10 Lincoln   50
11 Kaiser-Darrin   56
12 Mercury   58
13 Corvette   62

14 57 Chevy   66
15 Edsel   72
16 Thunderbird   78
17 Eldorado   84
18 Studebaker   90
19 GTO   96
20 Z-28 Camaro   104
21 Mustang   110
22 Shelby   116
23 Superbird   122

Index   126
Acknowledgments   128

MODEL T

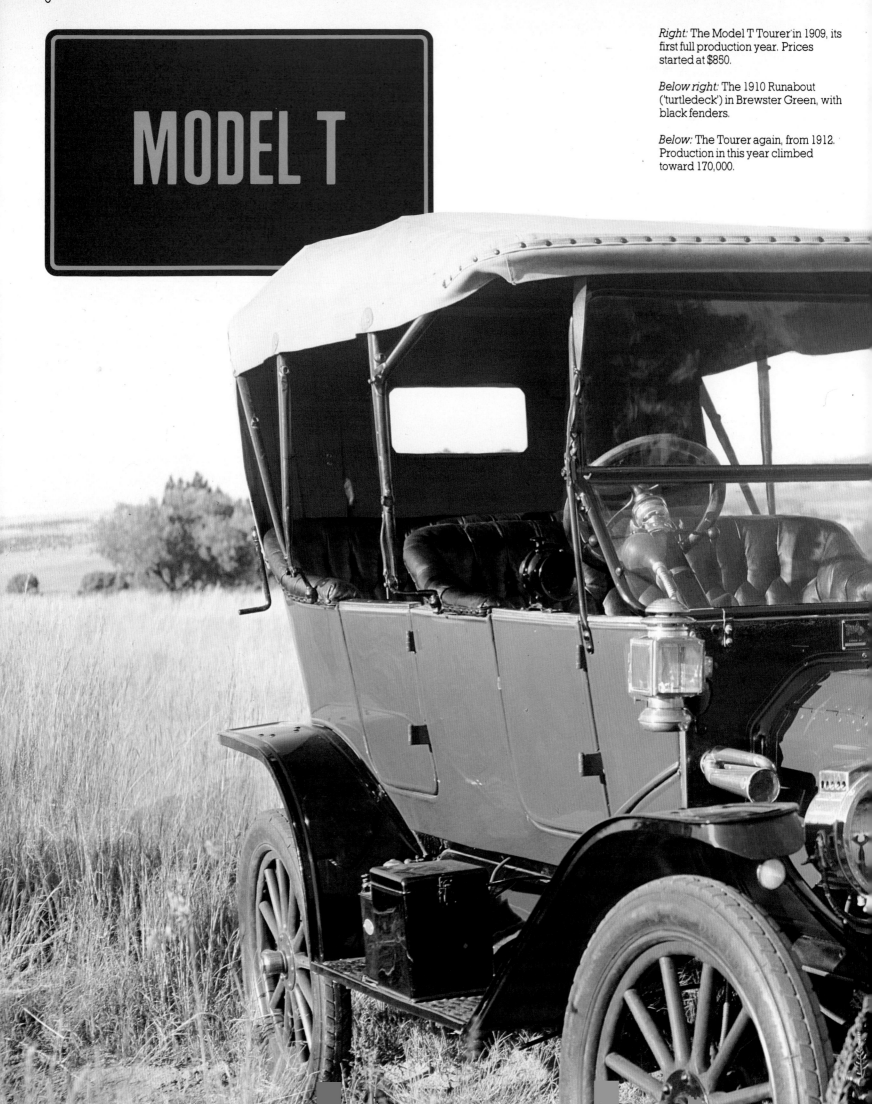

Right: The Model T Tourer in 1909, its first full production year. Prices started at $850.

Below right: The 1910 Runabout ('turtledeck') in Brewster Green, with black fenders.

Below: The Tourer again, from 1912. Production in this year climbed toward 170,000.

Up until the 1950s and 1960s when the growing use of automation lent a whole new meaning to the phrase 'mass production,' the world's largest-selling automobile had been Henry Ford's Model T. Unlike the current situation, in which cars are designed, built and sold by computer-aided committees, the Model T was the product of one man's genius. The Model T was not his only innovation. Now accepted as commonplace, Henry Ford gave America left-hand drive, introduced the initial concept of mass production, established an eight-hour day for his workforce and offered a guaranteed wage.

For a man of such immense vision, Ford could also be remarkably prosaic. He said that his love affair with the motorcar began the day he fell off a horse, he told the buying public that his car was available in 'any color you like as long as it's black' and meant it. He is often quoted as saying that 'history is bunk,' although the remark which the *Chicago Tribune* attributed to him in 1916 was 'History is more or less bunk.' It is a subtle distinction, and one for which Henry Ford is unlikely to have cared very much.

Henry Ford built his first quadricycle at his home in Dearborn in 1896, and became manager of the Detroit Automobile Company only three years later. Ford departed after a disagreement with his partner, Henry Leland, and the source of their dispute was significant to both. Ford believed that the route to financial success lay through making and selling large numbers of cars at low prices and small margins. Leland, conversely, wanted to build a smaller volume of expensive, high-quality cars. Both went on to fulfill their ambitions separately.

Ford's second venture, The Henry Ford Company, failed in 1903, to be swiftly followed by his third and final effort. The Ford Motor Company as we know it today began production in the same year. Models A, B and C sold well, the Model N gave Ford security as it sold 10,000 models and after its success Henry Ford aimed to put his major ambition into practice. He visualized a lightweight, 20hp, four-cylinder car capable of carrying five passengers in comfort, to be built in such numbers and at such low cost that motoring would cease to be the exclusive preserve of the rich; everyone in America would soon own a car, a Ford car.

In 1908 Ford unveiled the sheet metal of his vision, the Model T. It made its first appearance at the British Motor Show in Olympia, London, and was an instant hit – 250 were sold during the show. It was a four-cylinder, 20hp five-seater with a top speed of 40mph and was priced at $850 in its Touring form. It was also available as a Town Car, Runabout, Coupe or a Landaulet. Initially only Runabout and Touring were available, Touring in carmine red and Runabout in grey, although Brewster green was soon added, with a choice of dark blue or black fenders.

Production of the Model T began at the Ford plant at 254 Piquette Avenue, Detroit, on 1 October 1908. Ford's previous arguments with Leland had always revolved around price. Now, with the Model T, he would be able to test his belief that a small profit on each car would give it such a low selling price that it would boost sales enormously. Ford believed that the many small profits to be made this way would soon add up to a great deal more than a few big ones. History, bunk or otherwise, proves that his belief was absolutely correct.

However his pricing policy was also unusual for the time; on top

of the cost price 'extras' included headlamps (it had mounting brackets for them already), a windshield and a hood covering (top irons were included in the price but not the material).

The Model T sold a massive 17,000 units in its first year of production, which by itself was enough to give the new Ford Motor Company a guaranteed future. Only four years later production of the 'Tin Lizzie' was up to an incredible 170,000 – which would have been more than enough to make it a success story 50 years later, when Galaxie, Falcon and Fairlane were reaching similar figures.

As time went on and its manufacturing volume increased, Ford's theories were proved to be more accurate than perhaps even he had anticipated. The price continued to fall in directly

Above: A 1913 Runabout. Headlamps, windshield and hood were extras.

Left: A 1915 Tourer. The price is falling – the windshield frame is no longer brass, but black enamelled.

Right: A 1913 Tourer proves that the T did not have to be black.

inverse proportion to the production volume, encouraging still more people to buy a Model T, thus allowing the price to be reduced yet again. By 1916 the price of a Model T had fallen to just $360. Unbelievably, it continued its downward spiral and in 1923 hit its lowest ever price: a brand-new, straight from the showroom, any color you like as long as it's black, Model T Ford cost $260 – $590 *less* than the day it had been introduced 15 years earlier. It would also finish the year with a record production run of no less than 2,000,000 units.

Although the Model T established the basic parameters of the auto industry for the future it could not truly be called an automobile of any great genius or distinction until it was on the road. Its 2.9-liter four-cylinder engine introduced a small number of new features (like a monobloc engine casting with bolt-on cylinder head) and also used a number of 'borrowed' ideas like the Lanchester flywheel magneto. But it did display more than a few peculiarities of its own to the driver. The planetary transmission involved the use of separate pedals for forward and reverse instead of a gear lever. Coupled with a throttle which doubled as a brake (press to go, lift off to stop) and an advance/retard lever mounted on the steering wheel, the Model T was never an easy car to drive. In fact it was so complex that some states issued separate driving licenses for Fords.

The left-hand pedal worked the gears – down for low, somewhere in the middle for neutral and let it up for high. Reverse was engaged by pressing on the middle pedal, while the remaining one operated a transmission brake. There was an additional operating lever beside the driver; pulled back it engaged the parking brake and selected neutral by freeing the transmission clutches, pushed forward it released the brake and engaged the clutches. It was also unusual in being a left-hand drive configura-

tion, but there were so many of them built and in use that eventually this format had to be adopted as the norm throughout the USA.

However the Model T was still remarkably efficient in practice. The roads of the time were hardly more than dirt tracks, and it was well suited to them. Its lightweight frame, made from steel channel, flexed in response to rough surfaces and complemented the work of the rather rudimentary suspension of the time – its transverse leaf springs had no form of shock absorber at all. But its unsprung weight was low. The 30-inch wooden spoked wheels weighed very little, and they also afforded a high (10-inch) ground clearance, which was important at the time.

The early cars, up to about 1911, were bodied in wood shaped over wooden struts, finished with half-round molding at the joins. Later there came a growing use of metalwork, as the effort to cut costs became more and more frenzied. The leather interior was slowly reduced in quality, and eventually the leather door trims were replaced by pressed steel. The brass content of headlamps was reduced until by 1916 they were all-steel. The brass windshield frame became steel in 1913, and by 1916 that famous brass radiator shell had been replaced with steel.

But what it achieved was the most important thing. Almost alone, the Model T wrought a social revolution across North America. It brought small communities previously isolated by a two-day horseback journey within easy reach of each other and of large towns. It mechanized the activity of city dweller and farmer alike. It was practical, reliable, adaptable and, above all, affordable. More than any other item, invention or product associated with the internal combustion engine, it was Henry Ford's Model T which dragged the Western civilizations into the 20th century. Production ended in 1928, 20 years and more than 15,000,000 cars after it had begun.

Above left: By 1921 headlamps and radiator shell were no longer brass – but prices were still falling.

Above: A 1925 Tourer (with brass shell at extra cost!) developed 22.4hp from four cylinders.

Right: By 1927 the T had changed completely. Production ended in 1928.

STUTZ

Harry C Stutz built his first car – actually a gas buggy – in 1897. Then in 1905 he produced the very unusual American Underslung. As its name suggests, this had its chassis slung beneath the springs in an attempt to lower the center of gravity and improve its handling; quite what this did for unsprung weight is perhaps best left unexamined. Although drastically different, it was probably not the best solution to the handling problem with which all auto makers were wrestling, and Stutz continued his pursuit of the right answer. He did find it; a low frame allowing high cornering speeds was the crucial factor which enabled the Stutz Black Hawk to give the all-conquering Bentleys such a run for their money at Le Mans.

Harry Stutz had formed his company as a maker of motor parts, and it was the need to demonstrate the ruggedness of his rear axle under harsh conditions which prompted him to build a car to enter the very first Indianapolis 500, in 1911. The car ran faultlessly and finished an extremely creditable eleventh, which was a tribute to the axle and also to a variety of other makers' parts.

Like many other makers of small cars of the time, Stutz adopted a production technique which had as its end result what were known as 'assembled' cars. The brand company made some parts themselves and bought in anything else they needed to complete the vehicles. Ford, for example, bought engines from the Dodge brothers, and Henry Leland began his life in the auto industry supplying Leland-Faulconer engines, principally to Ford.

The engines used in the early Stutz cars were initially Wisconsin T-heads, although by 1913 they had been dropped in favor of Stutz-built powerplants of four or six cylinders. With these, Stutz racing performance improved considerably, and they came third at the 1913 Indy, a better result and a better advert.

The year 1914 saw the advent of what has since been regarded as one of the all-time classics, the Stutz Bearcat. This was a four-cylinder car with a 6.5-liter capacity, massive by modern standards but comparatively small for a four-cylinder in those days of piston-area theory. It was a T-head configuration, and developed some 60hp at 1500rpm. It was this car which sparked off the great rivalry between Stutz and Mercer owners which lasted for years.

In part this was due to the recognizable Stutz styling. Harry was an engineer rather than designer, and some of his cars were a trifle ungainly in appearance. But not only were they stubby in looks, they were also rather coarse, even brutish, to drive. Mercer owners, their only serious home-grown rivals, coined the insult 'you have to be nuts to drive a Stutz.' By way of retaliation the Stutz owners made up their own verse: 'there never was a worser car than a Mercer.'

The Mercer fans had a fair amount of truth on their side, since there was no question that the Mercer Raceabout was a far handier car than the bigger Stutz. However the extra power which their size accommodated paid off handsomely, and Stutz won more races than Mercer.

In 1915 the first full Stutz racing team appeared, known as the 'White Squadron' thanks to all-white livery and white racing coveralls. They were placed third, fourth and seventh at Indy that

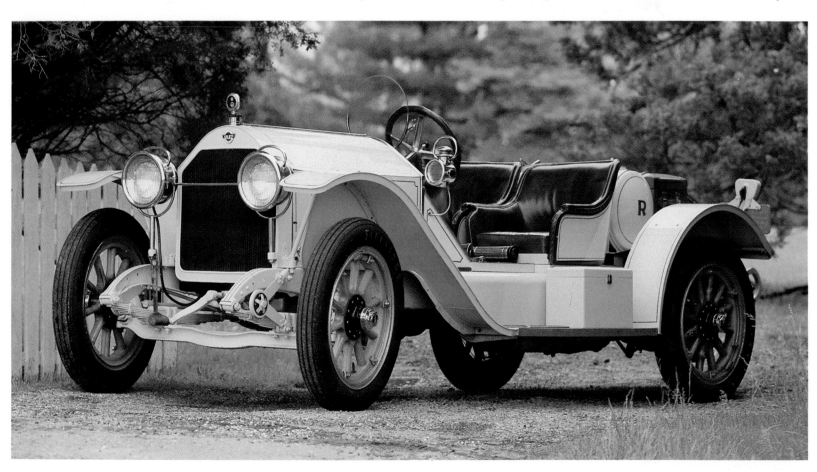

Above: The Bearcat from 1916, with monocle windshield mounted to the steering column.

Right: Cockpit and driver's controls and instruments from a 1914 Roadster.

Left: A 1914 Roadster. Amenities for driver and passenger were minimal.

Left and below: The 1920 Bearcat, with full windshield and all-weather hood.

Right: The impressive-looking DV 22 from 1933 – just two years before the company closed down.

year, an even better result than before, backed up conclusively when they won a selection of other events across America during the season.

Then in 1916 a disappointed Bearcat owner complained to a Stutz dealer that smaller-engined Mercers were much faster and were consistently beating him. The adverse publicity this generated, as the rivalry between the two makes was rising to ever greater heights, was considerable. Harry Stutz chose to reverse it in a marketing master-stroke easily worthy of anything current media experts could dream up.

Although there were few real roads anywhere in America at the time, this so-called 'lemon' was passed to a racing driver for a massively publicized attempt on the coast-to-coast record, then held by a motorcycle. Both the Bearcat and its driver passed into legend, and the driver gave his name to an event infrequently and illegally revived by Brock Yates. 'Cannonball' Baker scorched across the American heartland in 11 days, seven and one half hours; apart from the record, he broke only a shock absorber clip along the way.

In 1919 Harry Stutz parted from the company which bore his name, going on to build an uninspiring and rather unsuccessful vehicle called the HCS. After a short period under the control of Charles Schwab, Stutz was taken over by Frederic Moscovics, another engineer whose ambitions lay in a rather different direction to those of the firm's founder. Moscovics' stated intention was a concentration on 'safety, beauty and comfort.' The first car produced under his rule was a four-seat tourer known as the Safety Stutz, powered by a 4.7-liter straight eight with a chain-driven overhead camshaft, giving 92hp at 3200rpm. The chassis was a low-slung device, whose small ground clearance was the only real benefit produced by the use of a worm-drive rear axle. The brakes were likewise unusual, being quite literally hydraulic,

using water and alcohol-filled bags to press the brake shoes up against the drums.

On the same chassis came another nostalgic name, this time a two-seater christened the Black Hawk. This was closer to the old Stutz ethos, being based on Frank Lockhart's 3-liter land-speed-record car which Stutz had built and which had taken the American Class D record at 198mph. Later the racing developed again, and it was a different version of this which did so well in the 1928 24 Hours at Le Mans, although in 1929 it could only manage fifth place. In the 1928 event, though, the Black Hawk came extremely close to ending the domination of Le Mans by WO's Bentley Boys, splitting the pack neatly for second place. Had it not been for a lost top gear at 2.30pm, just 90 minutes before the end of the race, the Stutz may easily have come better than second. As it was, 'Babe' Barnato just managed to hang on to his lead, but the crippled Black Hawk still came ahead of the other two 4.5-liter Bentleys. It was the best placing for an American car so far in the event and would remain so for another 38 years, until the string of victories which Ford's GT40 began from 1966 onwards.

For 1930 the Blackhawk was improved, the engine growing to 5.25 liters and switching to Lockheed hydraulic brakes. It is a frequently heard rumor that 24 blown Black Hawks were built especially to take on the Bentleys at Le Mans, but apparently none has survived, if they were ever built.

The following year the extra power needed to make the cars competitive was achieved without a supercharger, but was found from the use of new cylinder heads. This dual ohc engine was known as the DV 32; it had four valves per cylinder and was fitted to a variety of different models, including the new Bearcat Torpedo Speedster and the 1933 Super Bearcat.

This still rather stumpy-looking two-seat convertible was the end of this stage of the Stutz story, and by 1935 they had stopped making cars altogether. It would be more than 30 years before the name would reappear on the street, although by that time the glamor of the 1920s would not be sufficient to compensate for other drawbacks.

Based on New York's Fifth Avenue, Stutz reappeared in 1969,

hoping to revive what was probably the best-known name in the American auto industry during the 1920s. Unlike the attempts by Auburn to resurrect an old design on a new chassis, Stutz elected to take a similar path to Duesenberg and design a whole new body, although it used the 116-inch wheelbase Pontiac Grand Prix chassis as a base.

On top of that Stutz placed a body which can easily be described as stunning, eye-catching or unusual. But like the original vehicles which bore the Stutz nameplate, it can not really be said to inspire admiration on the grounds of beauty. Chrysler stylist Virgil Exner, responsible for many stunning show cars, and designer of the 1966 Duesenberg (which is very similar in appearance to the Black Hawk) combined original body parts with an up-to-date design in an attempt to mix the flavor of the prewar era with the style of the 1970s. Built in Modena by Carrozzeria Padana, the Black Hawk features a squared-off radiator shell, curving fenders and external, chromed exhaust headers.

Power for the Black Hawk comes from the Pontiac V8; first it was the 400ci version, then the 455 big block and latterly the small 403 unit. It needs power; at more than 5000lbs, it's a heavyweight. It has a matching sticker price, ranging from $22,500 to more than $100,000, depending on model (hardtop, convertible or limousine) and specification.

MERCER RACEABOUT

Below: The low-slung 1912 Mercer Raceabout.

Below left: The 1912 35-C Raceabout with wooden spoked wheels and monocle windshield.

Mercer fans had their own little sayings about owners of the rival Stutz. While it was not necessarily true to say that 'you have to be nuts, to drive a Stutz,' there can be no doubt that the Mercer had at least as many plus points over the Stutz as the Stutz did over Mercer.

In fact even at this distance it is still difficult to make a choice between them, and fans of both makes are still liable to be as enthusiastic about *their* marque as were those of 70 years ago.

The Mercers always seemed to be proportioned just right, when even the most ardent Stutz fan will admit to a certain clumsiness of appearance; the Mercer always sits closer to the road and that certainly contributes to its cleaner looks. There was a lightness of look which began at the heart of the Mercer, with a spare, light frame that flexed to absorb the road – frequent signs of repair on those few examples which still survive are by no means all recent. However, the frame was strong enough to give the Mercer more than respectable roadholding and handling for its time, and it could still hold its head up in certain quarters even today, despite the tremendous advances that have been made since then.

The cars were built at Trenton, in Mercer County, New Jersey, by members of two families, Roebling and Kuser. Both were financially secure enough to be able to indulge a desire for small cars of a sporting character then unavailable elsewhere.

Their first effort appeared in 1909, the Model 30-C Speedster. Like so many cars of the time it was 'assembled.' Few car makers of the day could set themselves up in business with a full production line, so tended to buy in most, if not all, of the components from outside sources and 'assemble' them to their own design. Most large auto makers followed the classic path laid down by GM, and simply swallowed up these component suppliers as time went by; those who did not (or could not) either vanished completely or got swallowed themselves.

So the first Speedster used a four-cylinder Beaver engine which was a long-lasting feature of the marque; when the L-head engine became available it was incorporated into a heavier two-seater designed by Erik Delling. Its extra power more than compensated for the extra weight (70hp now instead of 50hp) and the factory guaranteed that it would cover a mile in 48 seconds. Desirable though both of these vehicles may have been – and still

are – they were not the ones on which the Mercer legend rests.

Designed by Finlay Robertson Porter, the Type 35 Raceabout made its debut in 1911. It had a four-cylinder 300ci T-head engine and a three-speed gearbox (supplied by Brown and Lipe and soon replaced by a four-speed unit). The factory guarantee was a mile in 51 seconds, but the early racers of the time found ways to improve even this. Like a number of contemporary vehicles and some illustrious names after it (Bugatti, Cobra and Corvette, for example), the Raceabout came ready to race from the showroom floor. But enthusiasts found ways to make it go still faster, largely by lightening the reciprocating mass inside the engine. The heavy flywheel was a prime target, with much weight machined away, and piston skirts were drilled to lose still more weight. With some fairly basic engineering modifications the Raceabout was capable of covering a mile in a great deal less than 51 seconds. Later there was a tendency to replace the stock 300-inch engine with a much faster 450.

Basic is a good word to use in connection with this car. While proponents of the Model T speedsters had to do a great deal of work removing nonessential bodywork for racing, the Mercer owners were spared all that. The Raceabout had very little in the way of a body to speak of, as it came from the factory. There were no enclosures, no doors, no cockpit. Perched behind the (enclosed) engine, with the protection of nothing more substantial than a 'monocle' windshield, the driver (who was placed on the right side of the vehicle) could see easily the left front wheel.

Right: The 1921 Series 5 Raceabout (and the 1922 model, *below*) had changed considerably, with L-head engine, doors, full-size windshield and even electric starting.

While it made for tremendous accuracy in positioning, it also meant that this was no long-distance tourer; few people could put up with the wind buffeting for more than a few minutes at a time.

It was designed and built for racing, and it soon began to collect trophies, honors and a reputation. In 1912 Spencer Wishart won a 200-mile event at Columbus, Ohio, with a showroom stock Type 35, setting track records at intermediate distances along the way. Soon names like Barney Oldfield, Eddie Pullen and Ralph de Palma were associated with Mercer, and adding more records to its history. De Palma averaged 70mph during a 150-mile event in 1912, Eddie Pullen 87mph in a 300-miler in 1914.

Yet it was by no means a slick vehicle; brutal would be a better word. The accelerator pedal was mounted outside the rudimentary bodywork, with a carefully placed stirrup below it for the driver to rest his heel in. The footbrake, which operated on the propshaft, was noted for its inability to do much more than effect a temporary (and slight) reduction in speed, and heavy pulls on the handbrake were needed to actually stop the car.

The later version, the L-head of 1915, is properly designated as model 22-70, but is almost never described as anything other than the L-head. By now it had changed in outward character quite considerably, and was more or less a luxury limousine by comparison with early versions. It not only had doors, but also featured electric starting as well, and would soon gain a factory-fitted full-size windshield. By now it had changed to left-hand drive, and gears were operated by a centrally placed floorshift.

The nature of the car, and the company, changed even more in later years. After Porter left, and the last of the Roeblings died, the company was taken over by a Wall Street combine, who gave control to Emlen Hare. Under his leadership Mercers began to appear as six-cylinder tourers, and the racing ethos upon which it had been founded and thrived, was gone. Soon it was a company struggling for simple survival, it was in receivership by 1923 and it had closed by 1925. An ill-timed revival attempt in 1930 was doomed from the outset, and the name vanished. So did almost all of their cars. In view of the hard life which they were built for and, practically without exception, led, that is hardly a surprise. From a total production of about 5000 cars, fewer than 100 still survive.

PACKARD

Main picture: The Packard heyday; a
633 Roadster from 1929.

Inset: Hood emblem from a 1933
V12 with Dietrich coachwork.

The first Packard was built in 1899, supposedly as a result of a
disagreement between one of the Packard brothers, James, and
Alexander Winton. In 1898 Packard had bought a Winton car with
which he was dissatisfied. Winton's response was to tell him to
build a car of his own if he thought he could do better. He did – and
it was better. Packard went on to become one of the great names
of the American auto industry until Jim Nance sold them down the
river and into disrepute in the early 1960s.

The first Packard was a single-cylinder device and almost
immediately the cars began to gain a reputation for reliability and
excellence. In 1903 Tom Fetch made the coast-to-coast crossing
in a stripped-down 12hp single-cylinder Model F which became
known as 'Old Pacific.' The journey clipped two days off the time
set by a Winton in the first ever crossing of this kind, but still took
no less than 61 days!

The year 1904 saw the advent of four-cylinder Packards and the

success of a K type race car called 'The Gray Wolf,' which set records at Daytona and then finished in fourth place in the first-ever Vanderbilt Cup. These early Packards set a tone which would later be followed by Stutz, Mercer and the Frontenac Fords, but for the time being the concept of the purebred sports-car had not arrived. Consequently Packard's sporty models like the 1910 Thirty Thirty were sold as a 'Gentleman's Roadster' and found great favor with the merely affluent rather than the rich.

However, all that gradually began to change. The first signs came in 1915, with the strangely named Twin Six. A V12, it was well-made and good to look at, with a restriction to two-wheel braking its only real drawback. By the early 1920s Packards were *the* American car to own, with Lincoln the only other real choice and Cadillac coming up fast behind. By 1928 annual production had hit over 50,000 units – a more than fair figure for a car with this kind of reputation and price tag. But from being the choice of presidents and playboy millionaires to a fall from grace was only a short step for Packard. Just around the corner lurked the Depression, and it augured less well for the independents than for companies like Cadillac and Lincoln, which could call on all the corporate and financial muscle of GM or Ford.

Clever marketing was Packard's only hope of survival and they seized it with both hands, downgrading their range and their prices to produce cars with a wider appeal than previously. By 1935 they had developed the eight-cylinder One Twenty, a car which found popularity in a new market but which was regarded by existing Packard customers as 'dismal.' Exclusivity through price had been a mainstay of the company, and this was now being sacrificed for mass appeal.

By 1937 the straight eight had been replaced by an even cheaper straight six, the One-Ten, and production soared, from 6000 cars in 1934 to over 100,000 in 1937. At the same time they worked to restore their previous reputation as makers of elegant roadsters for gentlemen – a range exemplified by the exquisite Model 734 boat-tail Speedster of 1929/30 and characterized by their eight-cylinder-only policy and Samuel Packard's personal pelican emblem on the grille.

In 1931 Prince Eugene of Belgium had used two Packard Series Eights as personal transport for his trip across the Sahara desert, and throughout the early 1930s the company continued to offer a range of V12 cars, elegantly bodied by Dietrich. But it was beyond doubt the move into lower-price markets which kept Packard afloat and which was ironically preventing its return to former glories among the country-club set.

Despite this Packard arrived at the end of the 1930s with a full complement of up-market cars in their lineup, with some excel-

Previous pages: A 1930 Model 745 Deluxe Eight Double Cowl Double Windshield Sport Phaeton.

Right: A 1934 V12-engined 1106 Sport Coupe.

Below right: A 1929 Model 734.

Below: A 1933 1105 Coupe Roadster.

lent coachwork from Rollston and LeBaron to show. Perhaps the most equal among those equals was the work of Howard Darrin, and beyond doubt his finest effort on Packard's behalf was the convertible 120-based Darrin Victoria. Away from Packard, 'Dutch' Darrin has a reputation of his own, but this rakish sportscar must rank among his best-ever work.

World War II also saw the smaller independent companies in dire financial straits, but Packard protected itself well. It built among other things Rolls-Royce Merlin aircraft engines under license and emerged into the postwar years in a reasonably strong position. During the late 1940s Packard worked to the same marketing strategy which had helped it survive the Depression, and it suffered in a short time.

The main problem lay in the perceived exclusivity of the prestige automobile, which was if anything more important now than it had been before. While Cadillac had created La Salle and Lincoln had formed Mercury to become their financial buffer, Packard just made Packards. In the immediate postwar period then, there was no distinction in designation between the more expensive range and the down-market offerings. Not only that, but styling was all but identical, so there was no visual distinction. The impetus to buy an expensive Packard was small when it could so easily be mistaken for a cheap Packard.

Cadillac soon became America's prestige leader and has continued to occupy that spot ever since. Packard was faced with something of a dilemma. Wrong-footed, it attempted to revert to its original policy of making only formal sedans under the leader-

ship of Jim Nance. He wanted to create a new, youthful image for the company to achieve this, and made the almost incredible decision to renounce Packard's illustrious past. At his direction the company's priceless historical archives were destroyed and the parts which were maintaining older Packards sent to the junkyard.

After two years at the helm he merged Packard with the ailing Studebaker company, which was by then in worse financial trouble than Packard itself. Even so Packard produced an all-new car for 1955, which featured 'Torsion-Level' self-levelling suspension, a range of three new V8 engines to replace the straight-eight series and 'Ultramatic' transmission. Sadly, build quality for these cars was a long way short of what it ought to have been, and still further adrift from what Packard quality was expected to be.

Although most of these problems were sorted out for the 1956 cars it was really too late. The 1956 lookalikes were in fact very fine automobiles, but the 1955 cars had put most potential buyers off and the visual similarity between the two cars did nothing to reassure them. In 1956 Packard built only 10,000 cars and did not even have the financial reserves to contemplate production for the 1957 model year. Jim Nance resigned from the company when it was acquired by Curtiss-Wright as a tax loss to offset massive wartime profits.

Even so Curtiss-Wright's man in charge of Studebaker-

Packard, Roy Hurley, felt sufficiently interested to attempt several moves to keep the firm alive, moving production to the Stude-baker plant at South Bend. The resulting cars were immediately nicknamed 'Packardbakers' and slightly fewer than 5000 were built in 1957. In 1958 there was little to note outside of a gaudy and bizarre styling exercise based on Studebaker's Golden Hawk. With a total production run for the year which could not climb above 3000 units, Packard, once the most illustrious name in the industry, disappeared for ever.

Above left: A V12 Coupe from 1937; by now the Packard prestige was beginning to slip.

Above right: A 1938 1608 Rollston DC Phaeton, one of the more formal models.

Left: A 1953 Caribbean convertible, part of Packard's new, 'youthful' image.

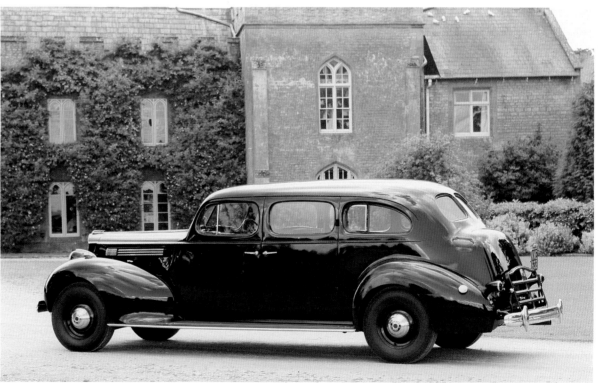

Right: The traditional Packard, a 1938 eight-passenger limousine.

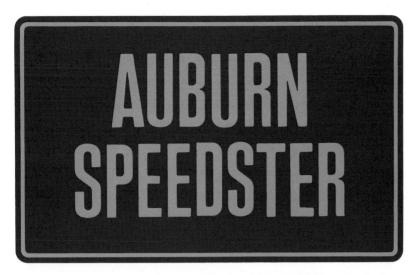

AUBURN SPEEDSTER

Like one or two other companies which took up the manufacture of motor cars after the turn of the century, Auburn began life as makers of fine carriages. The company was founded by the Eckert brothers at Auburn, Indiana, in 1876. They built their first car in 1900 and, despite a rather lackluster inventory, continued to exist – rather than flourish – right through the war years and onward. This was no small achievement in a period when the total number of auto manufacturers in the USA had dropped from about 150 to nearer 50.

By 1924, though, they were in real difficulties. Overburdened with debt, they lacked the financial muscle to dig themselves out of a deepening rut. Their highest ever production run in any year topped 5000 but in 1923 they had so many unsold vehicles on their

hands that they built only 175 cars. More by luck than anything else, Ralph Bard, the banker who controlled what was left of Auburn's assets, approached a Chicago businessman who had made a great success selling Stewart McDonald's Moon Motor Cars. Bard asked Erret Cord whether he would be interested in doing for Auburn what he had done for Moon.

Cord's inspection visit to the ancient and decrepit Eckhart Carriage Works is said to have made him laugh out loud. But despite that he struck a deal with Bard and with Auburn: they would give him a completely free hand, he would undertake the reconstruction of Auburn's fortunes but accept no salary. If he achieved the desired result then he would be able to buy the controlling part of the company's stock at a favorable price. No results – no sale, no deal. This rather daunting arrangement was the idea of Cord himself, the man who said 'success is obligatory.'

His first task as the new General Manager was to get rid of the existing stock, which he did by simply dropping the price, pitching it about $200 less than the comparable Buick instead of $200 more. In 1924, his first year of operations, Auburn sold 2226 cars – all old stock – while Cord set about revitalizing the range and bringing in new products. Initially confined to a sort of early customizing, the addition of coachlines and other cosmetic changes was replaced by a longer-term investment in Auburn's future. Cord persuaded Lycoming to begin work on a new eight-cylinder engine, and gradually began to increase co-operation and cross-pollination between Auburn and their component suppliers. Later on these smaller companies would be brought into the fold of the growing Cord empire as he added Lycoming, Stinson and then Duesenberg to his list of acquisitions.

By then the Auburn fortunes were climbing fast. Virtually out of debt by the end of 1924, the company was back into profit by 1925,

made an all-time record profit in 1926 and was paying share-holders a substantial dividend by 1927 – in which year 14,517 vehicles rolled from the factory. By now Cord had also brought the Limousine Body Company and the Central Manufacturing Company into the combine, establishing a new plant at the premises of the Lexington Motor Company (also snapped up) at Connersville, Indiana.

Aside from being a clever businessman and an accomplished engineer himself, Cord could also spot talent in others, and was quick to make use of it. He had employed Gordon Buehrig, Harry Miller and Count Alexis de Sakhnoffsky soon after he became President of the company in 1926.

While the first new Auburns (advertised as having 'the speed of an aeroplane, the comfort of your favorite armchair, the smart-ness of Parisian style, the luxury of a yacht and with the travelling certainty of the Century') Cord had overseen were lower, sleeker and smarter than before, they were by no means the best that was to come out of the company. Count Sakhnoffsky designed the body for one of the most elegant vehicles of the late 1920s and early 1930s – the 120 Speedster. This was a two-seat, high-speed

Right: The Auburn 'depression' cars were wildly successful. This 8-95 Sedan is from 1931.

Below left and right: It is the sweeping lines of the sporting Auburns which are best-remembered.

Above right: The 1935 Supercharged Auburn Speedster and hood emblem (*above left*).

Left: The 'boat-tail' 120 Speedster sailed through the depression years, and was guaranteed to be capable of 100mph.

sportscar which, like the rest of the 1929 lineup, benefitted from the arrival of the new Lycoming straight-eight powerplant. Pointing out that 75 percent of cars sold for less than $1000, Cord introduced the first $1000 Auburn, and by comparison to this 'cheap' car, the Speedster was priced at $1895 – not bad for a car which the advertising correctly claimed as 'holding many world's records.'

They were built as exact duplicates of a strictly stock car which had been handed to 'Mormon Meteor' Ab Jenkins. He had garnered the car's records when he streaked across the Bonneville salt flats at over 100mph for 12 continuous hours. The powerpack for this record setter was the Lycoming straight eight, mated to a well-tried and proven Duesenberg supercharger, although the production cars were also available without the blower. With it, each Speedster was sold with a written guarantee that it had been individually tested at 100mph, and a dashboard plaque to that effect.

This exceedingly elegant motor car was greeted with instant delight from all who saw it and remains a classic which is typical of the full-fendered grace and elegance of the period. It had another strong advantage in that once again Cord had got his pricing right; the Speedster cost a great deal less than did its major rival, the Stutz. This pricing structure, coupled with Cord's innate business acumen, probably accounts for the survival of the ACD empire over the next few awful years. Just as Cord had built his combine up to a point at which his future looked secure, it was threatened by circumstances completely beyond his control. The bubble burst one morning in October 1929 when the selling on Wall

Street began, and no manufacturer emerged from the Crash unscathed. Some did not emerge at all, which made Auburn one of the lucky ones.

With the rest of the ACD empire, Auburn survived the Crash and entered the years of the Great Depression; overall the early 1930s saw production in the US auto industry cut by 50 percent and more, although the balance was gradually re-established by about 1935. Cord directed his energies wholeheartedly into survival; he was well qualified and the industry at large had already seen the phenomenal results he could achieve when he concentrated his efforts in one direction. In 1929 production had been a record 23,297 units but sales fell sharply during the early part of 1930. Cord's response was typical; he improved the cars and dropped his prices. His 'depression cars' were a massive success. 1930 was another record year and 1931 beat even that, with 34,045 cars sold.

Having safely weathered the depression, the ACD combine finally failed in 1937. However, Cord himself still had Lycoming and assorted other interests and continued to prosper. Lycoming, of course, managed especially well as a supplier of aero engines between 1939 and 1945.

In the early 1970s the Auburn 120 boat-tail Speedster reappeared for a short while, on sale as a fiberglass body (from original drawings and specifications but based on a Lincoln chassis and a 427 Ford V8). Once again the company was catering to an exclusive and well-heeled market, but vanished a second time, finally and without trace, after the death of Erret Cord in 1974.

DUESENBERG SJ

The Duesenberg Company was formed in 1912 to build racing cars on a professional basis, and their success at this led inevitably to the manufacture of road cars. The first was the Model A tourer, which appeared in 1920. Like all Duesenberg road cars the Model A was based on knowledge and expertise gained from racing. All their road cars were excellent examples of advanced engineering, and quickly established the same superb reputation as the race cars had, quite literally, won on the track.

The Model A was light, using a good proportion of aluminum in its construction, and featured the Duesenberg's innovative four-wheel hydraulic braking system. With a 90hp Duesenberg straight-eight powerplant it was also fast and nimble, if overpriced. However the racetrack success which the marque continued to enjoy ensured that there was a demand for their exclusive road-going product. They were at the top of a small field; only the extremely wealthy could contemplate ownership of their cars. Although this may sound enviable it is not a recipe for financial security, and the Duesenberg brothers soon found themselves part of the empire which EL Cord was busy building for himself. From Cord's point of view it was a sensible decision, rounding out a portfolio which included the dramatic up-market styling and sensible pricing of Auburn, included Lycoming and its development work on a straight-eight engine and Cord's own plans for a car bearing his own name.

Duesenberg gave him instant access to the sort of clientele who lived in the area around his new Beverley Hills winter home. His first act was to give Duesenberg a blank check with which to build the fastest road car available to the American buyer. Fred's engineering expertise was widely recognized, but August, known as Augie, was himself an excellent designer. The combination of these two skills and Cord's driving ambition came in 1929 as the superb Duesenberg Model J. It was indeed a fine

The Duesenberg brothers, Fred and August, were German-born, and arrived in the United States as children. Like so many, their initial contact with the automobile came via the racetrack, although Fred's engineering genius had shown up very early on. They had turned this into practical value when they began to make bicycles in their home town of Des Moines, Iowa. The progress into powered motor racing was swift; the first engine was built at Rockford in 1898 and they built their first car in 1903. This began a long association with the racetrack which would link them with people like Eddie Rickenbacker and bring the marque a long list of racing success. Their victories at Indianapolis during the 1920s are well-known, and a Duesenberg became the first – and still the only – American racing car to score a victory in the French Grand Prix.

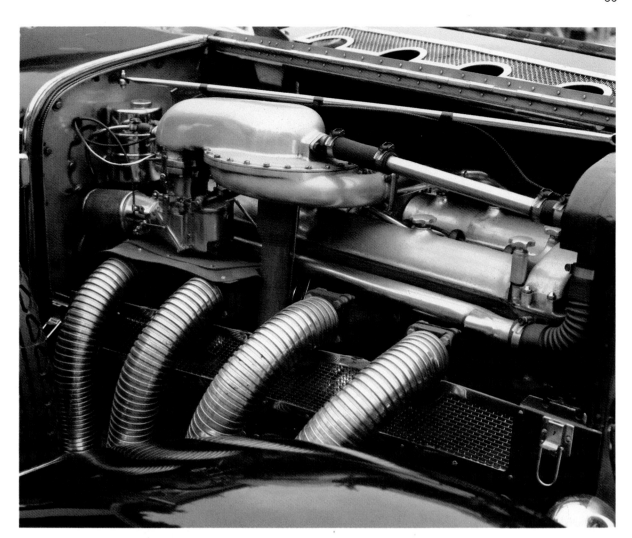

Right: Cord's blank check to the Deusenberg brothers produced the fastest road car in America – this engine is from a 1930 Roadster.

Below left: One of the original seven supercharged 1932 SJ Tourers by Derham.

Below right: A 1930 Model J Convertible Roadster by Murphy.

Left: A 1933 Duesenberg boat-tail Speedster.

Below and below left: Two examples of the DC Phaeton bodied by Le Baron.

Right: The most desirable of them all. In 1935 Duesenberg built two Speedsters to special order for Hollywood. One went to Al Jolson and the other – pictured here – was for Clark Gable.

automobile, with dazzling looks that easily matched its supercharger-boosted performance, and a price tag which also matched perfectly.

The basic powerplant was the newly developed Lycoming-built straight eight, with dual overhead cams and four valves per cylinder. It delivered a respectable 265hp, which gave the two-seat tourer an almost unusable top speed of 116mph. Even with full sedan coachwork, which could rival for looks even the best that Brewster and others were turning out for the Springfield-based Rolls-Royce America, the Model J could turn in a top speed of over 100mph. It fulfilled in every way the brief which Cord had laid down for it. The Model J featured chassis lubrication by an on-board oil pump, plus dashboard warning lights for oil and battery levels. It was also supplied without coachwork, and was still frighteningly expensive as an $8500 engine/chassis, but was sold all over the world, wherever there was anyone willing to pay more than $8500 for a car with no body at a time when the most prestigious Packard came complete for less than $6000.

The timing for the arrival of the new car could have been better; with the Wall Street Crash just around the corner the company was about to lose a fair percentage of the few people who could afford their prices. Without the security of the Cord organization around them the Duesenberg brothers would quite likely have disappeared along with so many of their contemporaries. However Cord's 'depression car' brought them through relatively

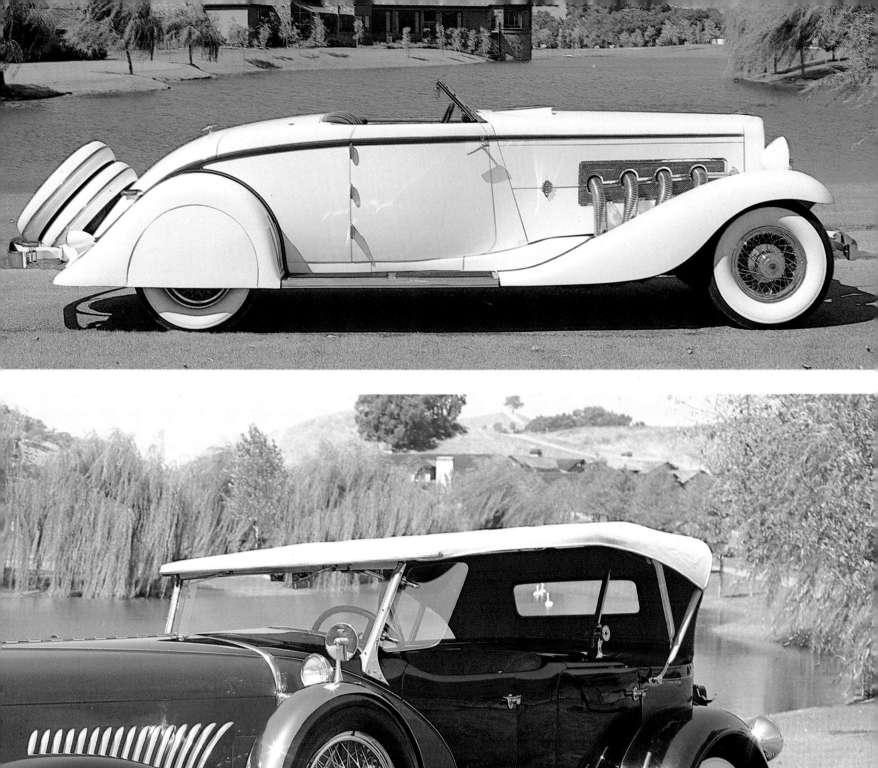

unscathed, and although a number of personal fortunes had been wiped out, many of those who had been rich enough to afford a Dusenberg before were still very rich.

Turning Auburn to the manufacture of cheap but good-looking cars for those who wanted to appear as wealthy as they had always been, Duesenberg directed their efforts towards providing automobiles for those who really were still very wealthy and wished to prove it. The Model J was thus replaced by the even more expensive and even more outstanding SJ, another supercharged design. Once again the design was full-fendered brilliance, and yet again Fred's engineering expertise had paid off; this was a car reckoned to be capable of about 130mph. The price was computed in fairly astonishing numbers too; a chassis with engine was priced at about $15,000 and coachbuilding could add almost as much again.

Fortunately Cord's belief that people able to pay for all this still existed proved correct, and on top of the chassis some of the leading coachbuilders of the day – Murphy, Le Baron and Derham – built some of the most classically elegant car bodies ever seen. Typically, their clients were royalty of some sort. They could be either the displaced variety, seeking to display wealth and status through their cars, or the newly grown Hollywood 'royals.' In truth there were few members of the Hollywood star set who could afford this sort of car, but those who could attracted interest and adulation on a worldwide scale: Clark Gable was one of Duesenberg's SSJ owners.

Having weathered the depression, the ACD combine finally failed in 1937; Fred Duesenberg died after a crash in 1932 and Augie made an abortive and unsuccessful attempt to revive the Duesenberg operation in 1947. Cord still had the Lycoming plant, though, and it continued to prosper, especially as a supplier of aero engines between 1939 and 1945. He died in 1974.

Right: 1935 supercharged SSJ. With a modified 448 straight eight, this is one of two built on a special 125-inch chassis, this one for Gary Cooper.

Below: A 1933 boat-tail coupe, rebodied by Waltham at the end of the decade.

32 FORD

Henry Ford had made himself a reputation on the racetrack with his handbuilt cars 'Arrow' and '999'; in fact race success with these was largely how he raised the backing to launch the Ford Motor Company. The huge quantities of his Model T which began to appear after 1908 meant that its appearance in motorsport was inevitable. There was truthfully no such thing as a sportscar at the time, and a Ford was as good a base as anything else. The early buckboard Ts were everywhere, racing on dirt ovals, the quarter-mile board tracks at county fairs, Pike's Peak – anywhere there was racing.

In those days the technique was simply to remove the body-work except the hood and a little cowl for the driver, who sat in a bucket seat bolted between the chassis rails. Engines were left more or less alone until Frontenac started a whole new trend, offering a 16-valve conversion for the 178-inch Ford engine. This was the first real performance option available for the production cars despite Henry Ford's sporting background.

The Model T was eventually replaced by the Model A, and then the Model B. This was a car which was designed to take the world by storm. Now regarded as one of *the* classic automobiles, especially by the hotrodding fraternity, the Model B stayed in production for only ten months and was something of a flop for Ford, although the reason was not that it was a bad car but that Ford was getting to grips with a whole new technology; there were no examples to follow and everything had to be thought out and tried out from scratch. The Model B arrived at a critical moment on the Ford learning curve and suffered as a result.

The Model B was late into production. As a 1932 car it should have made its debut in the fall of 1931, but it was not even formally announced until 1932 was several months old, although its arrival was expected, not to say eagerly awaited. When it did come it should have been available in a number of different body styles (up to 20, in fact), and for the first time Ford began to give them number codes, making the Tudor 700, the Roadster 710, the Fordor 730, and so on. It was also destined to have a choice of engines.

A brand new chassis made the Model B lower and stronger than the Model A, and its powerplant was essentially a Model A four-cylinder engine beefed up with a heavier crankshaft, which allowed it a higher compression ratio and a higher rev limit. In fact quoted output was up 25 percent, to 50hp. With rubber-bushed engine mountings and a new transmission with synchromesh on second and third, it was a faster, smoother, altogether more refined automobile, although for suspension it still relied on a single transverse leaf spring at each end.

The styling was also new for 1932. It was clearly based on the Model A, retaining among other things its 10-degree slanted windshield, but was swoopier and made maximum use of its lower profile which the new chassis, with a longer 106-inch wheelbase and curved, dropped rails, allowed. With one exception all of the Model A body styles were carried over, but 1932 was the first year that a 3-window coupe (designated 720) was offered: it was this which would become the Beach Boys' 'Little Deuce Coupe.'

Introduction was delayed, and the reason was the other new feature which made its appearance in 1932 and which would make its mark over the next 20 years – Henry Ford's new flathead V8. The Model B engine had been ready for production on time, in November of 1931. Problems with the V8 engine meant that it was not ready until much later. The *Detroit News* carried the first public announcement of the new car on 11 February 1932 and the first batch of V8 engines (just 18 of them) was built on 9 March. The first of the 1932 cars rolled off the production line on the following day.

Initial demand for the car was high, and an estimated 5,000,000 people called at Ford dealerships the first day it was on offer. But the problems involved in changing over the 32 assembly plants to handle the new model meant that the dealers had practically no cars to sell. By the end of March only 1220 engines and 1104 cars had been completed – and none of them were the four-cylinder Model B. Henry Ford had anticipated that demand for the V8 would outstrip the straight four by as much as three to one. However, as production problems with the new V8 delayed its manufacture, the four-cylinder engine was given a new starring

Overleaf: The Roadster is now the most popular of them all – less than 9000 were built. This one is the four-cylinder, 50hp Model B.

Right: The 'Deuce' lasted one year in production. Built overseas too (this is a British-built car), it had far more impact than the Dearborn figures might indicate.

Below: It's the 'V8' emblem which makes this a model 18 and not a Model B – also Clyde Barrow's favorite.

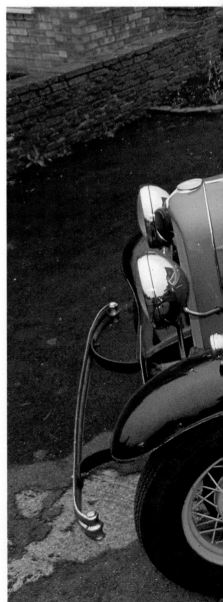

FORD

role in the lineup, and dealers were being forced to extol its virtues over the V8.

By the time production of the new car and engine had been placed on the right footing – a process which took several months – demand for the car had begun to wane dramatically. The all-time monthly high was achieved in June, when 42,904 V8 cars and 30,954 four-cylinders were built. But by then the effects of the Depression were beginning to bite home, and demand for all new cars was dipping downwards.

The last of the 1932 model year cars rolled off the production line in February 1933, and the total build had fallen well below Henry Ford's predicted 1,500,000 units. In fact they had made only 193,191 of the V8-engined Model 18 (to give them the correct designation) and 89,036 of the four-cylinder Model B. These figures include all of the various body styles. It was a smaller total than the number of Coupes alone which had been built in 1930, and included a mere 8996 Roadsters and 8870 of the superbly elegant Victoria models.

The Model B gained engine revisions and became the Model C in December of 1932, while the V8 cars were eventually transformed into the Model 40. Although the Model B utterly failed to live up to the expectations of either Henry Ford or his potential customers, there can be no doubt that it was, eventually, an excellent car. With the timing all wrong from the beginning to the end, it was eventually killed off by the Depression rather than by its own shortcomings.

If the car itself was no real success story then its engine was. The flathead V8 went on and on. It fulfilled all of Henry Ford's expectations, becoming the mainstay powerplant of the range for 32 years. Although by 1940 Henry had been persuaded to allow the introduction of a mid-range straight-six to compete with the offerings of other manufacturers, the V8 was *the* performance option, and the Henry Ford museum has a rather amusing testimonial from Clyde Barrow to back up its efficiency. Its major virtue was its immense strength; if anything it was over-engineered for the early 1930s, and, like the Chevrolet smallblock, it was capable of absorbing development as the years went by.

It stayed in production until it was replaced by the 130hp Y-block in 1953, and by then it was good for 110hp at 3800rpm. The Y-block was more powerful and revved higher, but even so the flathead was capable of still further development. Probably the greatest indication of its strength comes from the 'Ardun' hemi-head conversion which Zora Duntov designed. He realized that the engine had a terrifically strong bottom end, and that if all the power it contained could be unlocked then it could quite easily rev to 5000rpm without breaking.

Even without the Ardun conversion the flathead was still a performance favorite right up to the moment that the potential of Chevrolet's smallblock was realized, but even then the flathead had its fans. Its use in drag racing is still reasonably common-place, and no wonder. With the Ardun heads a blown flathead has clocked over 500hp, no mean figure by any standards.

CORD 810

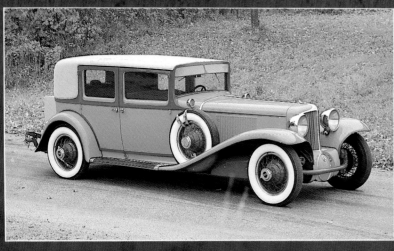

Left: The first car to bear Cord's own name, the 1929 L-29 Cabriolet.

Bottom left: A 1931 L-29. The short radiator shell and rounded valance reveal its front-wheel-drive configuration.

Below: 1936, the 'coffin-nose' shape of the 810 Westchester Sedan.

Erret Lobban Cord was born in Missouri in 1894, the son of a Scottish grocer. It was in Los Angeles that Cord came into contact with the automobile industry and soon discovered that he had a talent not only for cars but also for making money. His first venture began while he was still at college, converting Model T Fords into the stripped-down 'Speedsters' which were then the early form of sportscar and the car in which most motor racing was conducted.

This business flourished for him, and while building himself a reputation as a race driver of some skill he bought a service station and garage. He later invested his money in a trucking line which served the mining industries of Death Valley. It was the first real fortune he had made, and the first he lost. When the whole thing collapsed around his ears in 1919 the 25-year-old Cord headed for Chicago to start again.

His first job was selling the products of the St Louis-based Moon Motor Car Company. Using the same techniques he had learned with the Model T, Cord dressed them up with special paint, spotlights and assorted other tricks. Within a year he was sales manager of the company which had employed him. He continued

to sell more Moon cars than anyone else ever had, which enabled him to buy into the company fairly swiftly.

With such a brief and meteoric track record, it is no wonder that Cord was approached by the bankers who were facing heavy losses as the fast-fading Auburn company quietly drifted into obscurity and closure. Cord's remedies were swift and efficacious for all concerned; he put the company back on its feet, repaid the loans and gained control of it for himself. He was 32.

What followed is a classic tale of empire building, an outline script for the American Dream, and similar in almost every way to the rise of GM's William Durant. In a parallel of the acquisitive 'Magic Billy,' Cord began buying control of the myriad small component firms which supplied Auburn. Then as his resources grew, he went in search of bigger and bigger fish. He brought in Auburn's two main body-building contractors, then the engine suppliers Lycoming and finally the car-makers Duesenberg.

It was in 1929, by which time he was still only 35, that he gained what has to be the most exciting and prestigious reward the auto industry has to offer: he produced a range of cars bearing his own name. Fittingly, they were attractive, innovative and extremely successful.

For his own nameplate, Cord chose something which was even more spectacular than the attractive but traditional work he had been showing on behalf of Auburn and Deusenberg. The first Cord, the L-29, was a rakish sedan which featured America's first production front-wheel-drive system.

The technique was introduced by Walter Christie in 1904. Harry Miller patented the road-going version of a front-wheel-drive system he had been using in racing in 1929, when the L-29 appeared. It utilized a de Dion front axle on four quarter-elliptic springs. The car itself was designed by Carl van Ranst, and was lent extra elegance from the lower chassis and body which absence of a drivetrain permitted.

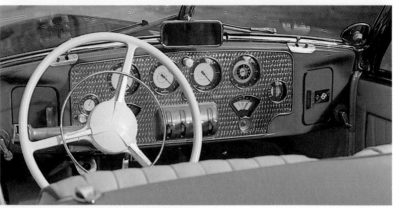

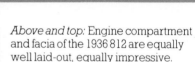

Above and top: Engine compartment and facia of the 1936 812 are equally well laid-out, equally impressive.

Above right: The Westchester Sedan is arguably at least as attractive as the convertible, possibly more so.

Left: A 1937 supercharged convertible with front wheel drive, independent suspension and concealed lights.

As he had done with Auburn, Cord wrote the advertising material himself. The brochure photography was all location work, done around the Beverley Hills area, where Cord had a house on Arden Drive. The Cabriolet was shot outside Harold Lloyd's front gate, the Phaeton outside the estate now owned by James Coburn, others near John Barrymore's hacienda. Exhibited in Paris and London, the Cord became an international success story, and in almost every country it became the transport of presidents, nobility and even royalty. Overseas distribution networks were established in 22 different countries.

Cord very smartly showed no pictures of the car when it was announced. His newspaper advertising was a mere announcement; interested parties *had* to visit a showroom to see it. The company was deluged with telegrams from overjoyed buyers after it went on sale, and the car very swiftly became an influential status symbol at country club and company headquarters alike. But the timing could not really have been worse.

When Wall Street woke up to disaster on 29 October 1929 many large companies, especially in the prolific auto industry, disappeared for ever. With a renewed range of 'depression cars' Cord hit a new high as a marketing expert. He sold cars which looked a million dollars for people who no longer had a million to spare. The technique was wildly successful, and the combine came through the worst years with record sales and rocketing profits.

With existing interests in Lycoming aircraft engines, Cord himself expanded his outside activities swiftly, taking advantage of the exceedingly uncertain stock market to buy his way into other companies in a series of classic boardroom coups. While his interests diversified, the company which bore his name launched a new car. If the L-29 had been a sensation in its time then the new

car was doubly so. It is the only American car universally recognized as a truly timeless classic. Now one of the most collectable cars in the history of the industry, the 810 series cars were still front-drive, but the body styling was at least ten years ahead of its time. The flood of congratulation which had greeted the first Cord was nothing compared to the praise with which the new one was greeted when it was announced in the fall of 1935.

With both Auburn and Duesenberg creating rakish sportsters of spellbinding beauty, the Cord 810 was still the combine's masterpiece, a pinnacle of excellence. Perhaps not as sleek as its stablemates, the 810 'coffin nose' was still a superbly good-looking car. Styled by Gordon Buehrig, its lines were clean and balanced rather than sweeping. The upright radiator shell was gone, replaced by wraparound horizontal gills, and not even the huge convoluted chrome headers which snaked out from the sides of the hood on supercharged models could detract from the lean economy of its styling. The streamlined effect was mostly due to another clever innovation – retractable headlamps in the leading edge of the front fenders, an adaptation of aircraft landing lights.

The 810 was also the first car to combine front drive with independent front suspension. However, this, combined with the powerful Duesenberg-supercharged engine, led to pronounced wear in the hub bearings. Production problems, especially with the transmission, which featured a mixture of electromagnetic and vacuum-operated gear change, meant that the 810 was never built in large numbers. Very few genuine 810s survive today – making them even more collectable.

However, with all that going for it, the 810 was not destined to last. Erret Cord returned from Great Britain, where his travels had taken him, to supervise the final winding-up of the ACD combine in 1937.

BUICK Y-JOB

Soon after he had been placed in charge at GM after their bankers had once again – and finally, this time – ousted the mercurial Billy Durant, Alfred P Sloan recognized that as advances in engineering methods brought the nature of individual cars closer together, the appearance of a car would be increasingly important, even critical, to its success. It was Sloan who created a department then known as GM Art and Color, and made the decision to employ the auto industry's first full-time professional stylist – Harley Earl.

His family business had long been coachbuilding, and it had grown with the automobile revolution at the turn of the century. It included custom-built car bodywork by the time the DuPont company had invented their first synthetic paint, 'Duco.' The business was much helped by its location in Los Angeles, and early connections with the movie industry led Earl into undertaking commissions for a number of the creative *glitterati* of the time. They were looking for something exotic with which to point out their difference from society at large, and they could not have found a more able or talented helpmate than Harley Earl. In a number of cases the working relationship blossomed into friendships which Earl kept up all his life; friendship with people like Cecil B De Mille and Al Jolson. These theatrical influences remained with him all his working life; for example Earl was the man who introduced sculptor's modelling clay to Detroit. He brought it from the design departments of the movie studios in Hollywood and revolutionized automobile design on the spot. Up till then Detroit's styling models had been made from wood, which may account for the angular nature of the product. Clay gave the designers more freedom to work with curved shapes. Earl formulated the process of evolving a new car through the stages of drawing and then model-making which remains normal today, and his clay process is only now being replaced by computer 'models.'

His fascination with the curved imagery of speed and function is well-known. Known throughout the industry as 'Misterearl,' his love of fighter aircraft indirectly gave Detroit the curved windshield, and the tailfin craze which he started with the 1948 Cadillac was reputedly sparked off by the twin-boom design of the P-38 Lightning fighter. During the late 1950s and early 1960s the extent of Earl's influence had extended beyond GM to cover virtually everything built in Detroit.

A large part of any designer's life is necessarily dedicated to the creation of designs which will never see production. The auto industry uses these 'dream cars' to help increase public perception of their abilities and far-sightedness as well as to pave the way for imminent design changes and innovations. Before television gave massive and instant public access, Harley Earl created the

Motorama shows for GM as a vehicle for his own work. The Motorama shows were a travelling circus which took the latest models and the current dream cars on tour across the USA, giving millions the chance to see – and buy – the latest from the styling studios.

Harley Earl was largely responsible for this himself. He stage-managed the change from Art and Color to Styling, a department specifically concerned with the production of dream cars, and gave the industry a new word into the bargain. His personal stock had risen to unassailable heights in 1936, when King Edward VIII had ordered a Harley Earl-designed Buick for State occasions. So it was naturally to GM's Buick division, rated second behind Cadillac, that Misterearl turned when he created his first dream car for public consumption rather than internal usage.

Prosaically known as the Y-Job, the car was drawn by Edward Snyder; it was Earl's practice simply to oversee and advise, and his styling 'clinics' were conducted from the comfort of an armchair, from which he would advise, suggest and criticize the efforts of his staff. The Y-Job was a two-seat convertible sportscar based on a stretched Buick chassis which gave it an overall length close to 20 feet. Earl had already expressed a great deal of what was in store through the 1934 La Salle, and the Y-Job continued this theme. It also included some elements of Chrysler's ill-fated but admirable Airflow, but still managed to demonstrate styling techniques which would not make production for another ten years. One of Earl's biggest problems was running slowly; he

often found it difficult to pace himself to a point which was only slightly ahead of current public opinion.

The Y-Job was a perfect blend of three-dimensional curves, and although it used an enormous amount of sheet steel it looked like a lightweight. Earl's strategy was based on making his cars look longer and lower than others by styling tricks and the Y-Job is a perfect example of how well he succeeded on so many occasions. The car itself had power windows, concealed and power-operated headlamps and a power-operated convertible top which retracted into a special compartment behind the seats and ahead of the trunk. It had huge, solid chrome bumpers front and rear which were given a wraparound look by extended chrome fluting along the fenders, and it had a radiator grille horizontally aligned to blend in. Work on the car had begun in 1937, and it made its public debut in 1940. Saying it was well received is like saying that Frank Sinatra is quite a good singer.

However, it was not destined for a great deal of public exposure, and was in fact rarely displayed. Instead it became Earl's personal transport, and he used it mainly to make his frequent weekend appearances among Grosse Point society. After the war ended, though, the Y-Job was dusted off and emerged into the public gaze once more. By now Earl had got the Motorama concept up and running, and despite the availability of production models and dream cars which had taken shape in the intervening ten years, the Y-Job not only stood up, it stood out, still as breath-takingly elegant as it has been in 1940.

LINCOLN

Left: A 1929 Lincoln Dual Cowl Phaeton.

Most people associate the name of Edsel Ford with one of the auto world's prize turkeys, but that was a car which was named after him. Conversely, Edsel himself was the motivation behind one of the most prestigious names ever to come from Detroit, through the creation of just one vehicle which made Lincoln one of the most desirable marques.

The Lincoln Company itself was founded by Henry Leland in 1917. He had already rescued Henry Ford's second auto company from collapse and renamed it Cadillac, before moving on to create Lincoln. So when Lincoln hit financial problems in 1922 there was a certain irony in the fact that Henry Ford snapped it up for $8,000,000 and then ignored all his promises to leave Leland in control; he was simply dismissed. Ford then passed control of his new acquisition to his son Edsel; Ford's own attention was fully

Right: Lincoln Continental Cabriolet. Production had just got into full swing for this 1942 model year when it had to halt.

Below: The V12 Lincoln-Zephyr was available in 12 body styles, of which the Continental was just one. The bulk of sales were concentrated on the four-door Sedan range like this from 1937 and the 1940 model (*inset*).

occupied by the Model T. Edsel said that while his father made the most popular car in the world, he planned to make the best.

After the Wall Street Crash, however, Lincoln's sights had to be dropped somewhat, and their products owed more to Ford than to any other influence. Then the Briggs coachbuilding firm showed a car which had been designed by John Tjaarda; Edsel saw it as a new small Lincoln which would uplift the company's fortunes, and after revision to accept a new V12 engine the well-received Lincoln-Zephyr was born.

It was on this successful base that Edsel decided to have a personal car built for himself in 1938. He asked Bob Gregorie, whom he had appointed head of the styling department he had created in 1932, to handle the styling for him. But it was Edsel's major instruction to 'make it as continental as possible' which set the tone for the new car's appearance and gave it a name which was to become synonymous with everything that was best in a formal sedan.

Gregorie fulfilled his task accurately, although it was again Edsel who added the finishing touches to its styling. He insisted that an externally mounted spare wheel carrier was an essential part of 'being continental.'

Edsel's 'one-off' personal car included a 12-inch stretched Zephyr hood and chopped-down Zephyr doors on a specially built chassis. The rest of the body was handmade to Gregorie's 1/10-scale clay model, and the result was an elegant, well-balanced shape destined to be a classic, proving once again that a car designed and handbuilt to fill one man's dreams is generally better looking than anything mass-produced to meet a hundred thousand motoring needs.

Lincoln power was standardized on the 266ci L-head V12 introduced for the Zephyr, which at its introduction delivered 110hp at 3600rpm. It also gave maximum torque at an incredible 400rpm, making it almost strong enough to scale vertical inclines, and making the gearbox a virtually redundant irritant. Unbelievably, the three-speed transmission also featured an overdrive facility, operated by a control on the steering wheel and effective at speeds over a very low 20mph.

By the time Edsel's personal car was ready (he had specifically asked for it in time for his vacation) the output of the V12 had been improved to 120hp, and with this sort of power on tap he set off on his annual pilgrimage to Palm Beach. The car created such an outstanding impression among Edsel's well-heeled friends that he returned with over 200 orders for the car – which was now to be called the Lincoln Continental.

Edsel himself had been so pleased with the car that he had already ordered two more for his sons Henry Ford II and Benson, but now it went into full-time production – as a handbuilt item. Offering the old-time quality standards which had been slowly vanishing since the Crash, the Continental was scheduled for a limited build of 500 units; 200 to satisfy the friends who had seen the car at Palm Beach and the other 300 for those others of Edsel's friends and contemporaries who could afford it. By late 1939 only 25 of them had been made; production had to be stepped up for 1940. Using the slightly shorter sheet metal for the 1940 model

year Zephyr, 404 Continentals were made, 54 coupes and the rest cabriolet versions.

Then in 1941, with only minor detail changes, the Continental really caught on. In the same way that sight of the original had provoked 200 orders, the 500 now in circulation sparked off yet more. Again these came from people who saw it and could afford it, and the Continental was well established as an exclusive means of transport. America liked it enough to double output again, and they could afford it too. There were 400 cabriolets and 800 coupes (the only two body styles available) built, and sold, in the 1941 model year.

Almost certainly its success would have continued to grow in 1942, even though its appearance altered substantially. The styling changes squared up its appearance, making it look heavier and more cumbersome than Edsel's original. In fact that was the truth of the matter rather than a mere impression, for it was about six inches longer and most of the extra length was overhanging chrome. The new bumpers were much bigger than before, and the almost delicately scalloped grille on the original had given way to a more traditional but heavyweight arrangement. Engine capacity was also increased in 1942, going up to a modest 292ci, and taking the power up a small step to 130hp – which was respectable enough at the time.

This year only 336 Continentals were made; in 1942 the United States were fully involved in World War II, not a year of optimism likely to provoke sales of luxury automobiles. It was the year in which the Detroit production lines were turned over to the

Top: Original Lincoln advertising for the new 1949 cars.

Above: The postwar Continental was a carryover from the 1942 dies up to and including the 1948 models.

Above left: Facia was remarkably straightforward. This is a 1947 Continental.

Left: It was the spare tire location outside the trunk which Edsel Ford felt was especially 'Continental.'

Top right: Front view of that 1948 Continental Convertible.

production of war materiel – the very thing which Leland's original Lincoln Company had been formed to do and the cessation of which, in 1918, had brought him to Henry Ford's doorstep with an empty bank book. In World War II, though, it was the Ford empire which churned out a huge quantity of vital supplies – at one time the Willow Run plant was making a complete Liberator bomber every hour of the day and night.

In 1943 Edsel Ford died; he had taken over control of the entire Ford empire from his father in 1941 after an ugly power struggle and a number of decisions and actions on the part of Henry Ford which onlookers found surprising to say the least. It had ended when Henry Ford suffered a stroke, but after Edsel's death the 80-year-old Henry resumed his post as President and Chief Executive for a short time. Henry abdicated in favor of Henry II in 1945, and it was left to his grandson to resurrect the passenger-car business when the war was over. Like the products of practically every other Detroit auto maker, the 1946 Fords were little more than revitalized 1942 models – and that included the Continental.

Both prewar models went back on sale in January 1946 – the cabriolet now termed a convertible coupe – at fractionally more than $4000. This was little more than they had cost when production halted in 1942.

Still powered by the 130hp V12 mounted in the same standard 125-inch wheelbase, they were, however, missing most of the vulgar brightwork of the time, and simply bore their name in script lettering on the hood. The most noticeable change which distinguished the prewar Continental from the 1946 model was the thick-barred egg-crate grille. Some 446 were produced in the first full year after the end of hostilities, almost evenly split between coupes and convertibles. In 1947 the Continental enjoyed its most successful sales year so far, as another almost even split of coupes and convertibles ran to 1569 units. Sales were nearly as good for the unchanged 1948 cars, but this time the 1299 units were biased in favor of what were now called club coupes – nobody wanted the convertibles.

Production of the $5000 car was halted before the end of the year as Ford energies were concentrated once again on low-price, high-volume production. At the time Ford itself only sold one car in its entire range which cost more than $2000, and there was little room for the handbuilt Continental in the bustle of the postwar boom. With shorter wheelbases and cars which were altogether more practical, Lincoln enjoyed poor to middling fortunes through the next decade. But in 1961 the company produced a car of such elegant styling that the design team won an industry award, and the Continental name, now indelibly established as belonging to a marque of superlative style and excellence, was resurrected and fixed to a Lincoln hood. Even this luxurious sedan, though, was no match for its illustrious forebear.

KAISER-DARRIN

In 1942 Henry J Kaiser wanted the American auto industry to start work on its postwar range, despite the fact that civilian effort was slowing to a stop to concentrate on war production. His reason lay in the fact that he himself was experimenting with plans to build cheap plastic cars after the war which would cost less than $1000. He had a massive lead, he felt, and was anxious to secure the advantage he was sure he possessed.

As early as 1944 he had signed deals to go into production with GRP (fiberglass) bodies after the war, and several prototypes were completed at the Kaiser laboratories in California. When the war finally ended Kaiser went into partnership with Joseph Frazer, although the cheap plastic car was no part of the plan. Instead, the proposal was for a unibody front-drive car with torsion-bar suspension. Production problems, plus the fact that the design was truthfully not that well integrated (it would have needed expensive power assistance to counteract its very heavy steering) meant that it was never destined to be. Instead the Kaiser-Frazer of 1947 was a lower-priced version of the conventional rear-drive Frazer.

Built at the Willow Run plant which Ford had used for wartime bomber production, the car was an instant success, and made the young company the ninth-placed (and best independent) in the industry. However, their fortunes took a nosedive in 1949 when the first real postwar designs from Detroit's big guns surfaced against a mere facelift for the Kaiser-Frazer. New models for 1951 restored them to 12th place, but after that it was a progressive downhill slide. By 1954 total production was down below 20,000 units, and in 1955 less than 1300 cars were built. The company wound up that year with a loss of no less than $100,000,000.

Yet the story could easily have been very different. By the early 1950s both GM and Ford were known to be looking at a cheap two-seat sportscar concept with which to fight the European imports dominating a market which had sprung up when the war ended. GM in particular were examining the possibilities presented by the extraordinary advances in plastics technology which had been accelerated by the wartime crucible.

One of the elements which had spurred Harley Earl into rejuvenating the Chevrolet project, and giving it much higher priority, had been the appearance, in 1952, of a small fiberglass two-seater designed by Howard 'Dutch' Darrin. It created a great deal of interest when it was first shown; Owens-Corning had worked hard on the development of fiberglass as a material for minesweeper hulls during the war. It was properly named Glass Reinforced Plastic (GRP) and had excited a great deal of interest in the postwar world, especially in Detroit. Darrin was the first person to show what looked like a practical, marketable automobile built in this new material.

He had been a designer of custom coachwork before the war, and had made the decision to go into production with a car of his own when the war ended. He had chosen fiberglass as the material for his pretty 2-seater convertible and planned for an annual volume of 30,000 units. His search for financial backing led him to the New York-based Lehman brothers, whose finance house had also been approached to underwrite the forthcoming alliance between Kaiser-Frazer. Lehmans eventually said no to both propositions, and although Kaiser-Frazer went ahead Darrin was not so lucky.

When the Darrin prototype appeared in 1946 it was powered by the 100hp Kaiser straight six. A rectangular box frame gave it a 115-inch wheelbase, with an overall length of 185 inches. Apart from its use of fiberglass it incorporated a number of unique features. A massive inbuilt hydraulic system was used to provide power for the operation of practically everything. Power seat adjustment was among the most commonplace, while power-operated convertible tops were not completely unheard of. But there was a four-wheel jacking system included, and the clamshell hood (which included the front fenders) could be raised by hydraulics to expose the engine and front suspension.

There was already an association between Darrin the designer and Kaiser-Frazer as manufacturers, so it was naturally to Kaiser-Frazer that Darrin turned when he wanted to put his next project into production. This time it was nowhere near so radical as before, although it was still a fiberglass-bodied two-seat sportscar. Its two doors were slid aside to open, rather than hingeing outwards in the conventional way, and the convertible landau top had a half-open position. Power for this also came from the

All pictures: Perhaps a little strange-looking to modern eyes, Howard Darrin's fiberglass sportscar (this is a 1954 production model) embodied some new ideas, like its sliding doors, and captured contemporary imaginations.

smallest of the engines Kaiser-Frazer offered that year. There were three engines available; a 226ci six of 140hp or 118hp, and the smaller 161ci Willys F-head unit which developed only 90hp. Darrin had chosen the smaller for his car when building an amazing 60-plus prototypes at his California workshop. Although the car was nimble, with its three-speed floorshift, its top speed was marginally below 100mph.

Priced at $3668, it was not cheap compared with imports like MG, Jaguar and even Porsche, nor to its new homegrown rival, the Corvette. Chevrolet had shown their dream car in 1953 and gone into limited production six months later. The Kaiser-Darrin was available for the 1954 model year and found a similar lack of welcome to that which nearly put paid to Corvette. Without the security of GM it is unlikely that the Corvette would have survived; Kaiser were already on shaky ground and could not support their own bread-and-butter range. Just 435 of the neat Kaiser-Darrin sportscars were built during 1954, and none appeared during 1955 as the company was wound up.

Dutch Darrin was understandably disappointed with the outcome, although he could see clearly where the fault lay; like the Corvette, his car was underpowered. Darrin himself bought around 100 of the uncompleted cars which were left at the factory when it shut down. He fitted them with Cadillac V8 engines – giving them a fairly astounding 140mph top speed – bumped the price up to $4350 and sold them easily from his Los Angeles showroom. With the strength of a bigger manufacturer behind him, Darrin's neat little car could easily have survived, and might easily have captured public imagination the way that Corvette did in later years.

MERCURY

Edsel Ford has somehow never emerged from the history of the automobile industry with the same kind of stature as have his father and his son. Henry was renowned for his innovation and for his clear-sighted ability to see the importance of the automobile long before any of his contemporaries. Henry Ford II was a clever administrator of the car giant he took over in 1945. He recognized talent and employed it well, even sought it out specifically. He also made sure that no one with genuine ability acquired more than a certain amount of power within the company, so they could not challenge his authority; he thus ensured that there were none of the ugly power struggles which had surrounded his cantankerous grandfather in the late 1930s. Under 'HFII,' as he was known, the Ford Motor Company grew in prosperity and in strength.

Edsel had the least appealing task of all. Working for so long in the shadow of a man revered by those around him as a genius, a man who had accumulated great power and did not always use it wisely, Edsel was given control of the company as it entered upon

production of military equipment. He died very soon after, and his father once again held the reins until HFII returned from his wartime activity in the Navy.

For the greater part of his working life Edsel Ford was restricted to a position which was very much that of second fiddle to his father's number one. In that unhappy situation he turned his attention to something he was in fact very good at: manufacturing excellent cars. When Henry Ford bought Lincoln from his erstwhile partner Henry Leland, it was left to Edsel to make it into one of America's premier car makers. It was Edsel Ford who clearly saw the need for the Ford Motor Company to have a middle-market competitor between Lincoln and their bread-and-butter range.

The Mercury was announced late in 1938 as a 1939 model, with Pontiac and Oldsmobile as its nearest main rivals. The series 09A came in five different styles, sized and priced between Ford and Lincoln, all on a wheelbase of 116 inches, all using a 239ci flathead V8 of some 95hp, slightly larger than the standard Ford powerplant. With more than 80,000 units in that first year (as against Ford's 500,000-plus output) it was nowhere near the massive GM figures but still placed about 12th in the industry – good enough to be called a first-year success.

Obviously the range drew heavily on Ford, and it was as evident in styling, where there was a pronounced family likeness in 1940, as in engineering. After a few small alterations there was a much more involved and chromier facelift in 1942, as well as the arrival of the new 'Liquidmatic' clutchless transmission. The war intervened at this juncture, and by the time it ended Edsel had succumbed to a stroke and HFII was left to preside over Mercury's operations. The 1946 cars were basically nothing more than a carryover from 1942, although plans for a whole new range existed.

Then in 1947 the corporate structure was completely reorganized. Up to that time Lincoln and Mercury had been little more than parts of Ford, but Henry Ford II created the Lincoln-Mercury

Left: The 1948 Mercury became a youth culture car almost immediately. The epitome of Californian cruising, the two-door cars (this is a 1950 model) are still on the roads.

Above right: Its smooth shape presented almost endless opportunities to the custom shops like Barris, and few survive in original trim.

Right: The distinctive Mercury 'jukebox' front end.

Division to run separately, along the same lines as the GM operations. The close alignment with Ford had been seen as a slight disadvantage to both Lincoln and Mercury and now that was changed things began to move ahead.

In 1949 the major restyle delayed from 1946 arrived, although slightly modified. Still large cars (on a 118-inch wheelbase), the 49 Mercurys had an altogether longer, lower and sleeker appearance which gave the models of the next few years an appealing look which still holds good. They became firm favorites among the hotrodders of the day and quickly established the traditional low-rider, lead-sled look which still persists as an essential part of the customizer's art.

All the American cars of the early 1940s had been restricted by the materials available (government regulations introduced in 1942 had limited the amount of chrome, for example) and there had consequently been a resurgence amounting to excess in the late 1940s when the restrictions were lifted. In general this would persist throughout the 1950s, but the 49 Mercurys were extremely clean-looking, with only a single chrome strip along each side. This general attitude was adopted by the customizers, and they took their activities in the opposite direction, making removal of all superfluous chrome a virtue. This would be reflected by Mercury themselves with cars like the 1952 Custom Hardtop, which even used body-color headlamp trim. This was part of a styling trend seen throughout the Ford range that year, during which the visual similarities between Mercury and Lincoln became more and more apparent.

For 1950 and 1951 the styling remained more or less unchanged, though, and that feeling of heavyweight elegance re-

Left: Ford's flathead V8 had ruled the performance roost since 1932. By the time it appeared in the early 1950s Mercuries it was reaching the end of life.

Right: This 1951, with Appletons and Lakes pipes (plus signs of lowered suspension), is not strictly original – but it is authentic 1950s nonetheless.

Below: The split-screen cars were on their way out, and this was to be the last year before the excesses of chrome and glass began to appear in Detroit.

mained. Most desirable of all was the 1950 2-door coupe, which made the 4-door seem just a little bit too fussy by comparison. Minor changes to its shape in 1951 were followed by the disappearance of the split windshield in 1952. This was replaced by a single piece of glass with a slight curve, which modern collectors see as being rather less desirable.

Under the hood little had changed. The 1949 models, with their 255ci, 110hp L-head V8, had been the first genuine 100mph Mercurys; they crept up to 112hp in 1951, getting a bigger boost to 125hp from a higher compression ratio to go with the 1952 styling clean-up. 1953 was the last year for the new shape which had appeared in 1949, and in any case its heritage was hardly recognizable. In 1954 Ford produced its new overhead-valve Y-block V8 together with some styling alterations and then produced an all-new look for 1955.

For the next few years the Mercury range had little to distinguish it, despite the fanfare launch of the new 'Big M' line by Ed Sullivan in 1956. Even the much-vaunted 1957 Turnpike Cruiser relied mostly on gadgets like 'Seat-O-Matic,' which adjusted the driver's seat to any one of 49 positions at a touch. Nevertheless the range continued to enjoy more than moderate success, joining the general move towards compacts after the middle-bracket market collapse which sealed the Edsel's fate in the late 1950s.

From then on Mercury was virtually relegated to providing up-market versions of Ford models – Meteor/Fairlane and Comet/Falcon are good examples. By a stroke of good fortune this left Mercury with a handy position when the musclecar era began to get into its stride, and names like the Comet Cyclone GT and Cyclone Cobra Jet 428 got a great deal of attention – especially after Cale Yarborough's win at Daytona in 1968.

Although by the mid-1960s Mercury fortunes were largely restored and its model base was back on traditional lines, there were still a few more names to conjure with in the pipeline. The Marauder X-100 was one such, although the best of the lot was their up-market, up-sized Mustang, which in 1967 appeared as the Mercury Cougar, Cougar GT, Cougar GTE and Cougar XR7 in the approved musclecar tradition. With 390hp on tap from its 427 V8 there was no doubt that this was a car to be reckoned with, and despite its Mustang allegiance it was also a good looker in its own right, especially in its early years. Although its sales never came near those of the Mustang there is no doubt that it was at least as much fun to drive, and the 1967/68 models are highly esteemed.

CORVETTE

There are few cars for which all superlatives seem inadequate. In most cases they are an exaggeration, often little more than pure puffery. For Corvette the picture is rather different, for here is a car which was and is genuinely innovative, which has established industry firsts, precedents and standards, which has lasted for more than 30 years and in that time has risen from being America's first and only real sportscar to its present position, where it is America's first and only supercar. No wonder it is held to be a legend in most motoring circles.

Zora Arkus Duntov is generally referred to as the father of the Corvette, and is equally often, but mistakenly, credited with its design as well. But when Corvette was on the drawing boards of Chevy styling Duntov was still enjoying a career as a racing driver, winning his class at Le Mans for Porsche. He joined

General Motors in May 1953, five months after Corvette had first been shown as a concept at the New York Autorama and a scant month before Job One rolled off the production lines in Flint, Michigan.

However, Duntov did go on to have a tremendous influence over future Corvettes, and was responsible for a great deal of the development work which made it the superlative car it eventually became. Initial Corvettes enjoyed as their sole source of power Chevrolet's ancient, almost antique, stovebolt six, an engine designed in 1929. Budgetary requirements dictated this course, as they also dictated the choice of a miserable two-speed automatic transmission, and it was left to Chevrolet engineers to make the best of them. Even with some extra power, the straight six left Corvette extremely underpowered, and it did not really sell well until the arrival of Ed Cole's brilliant smallblock V8 – Chevrolet's first for more then 30 years – in 1955.

Planned to combat the supremacy of the Ford flathead V8 which had first seen service in 1932 and was still going strong, the V8 was a natural choice for Corvette. When Duntov gave it first a wild camshaft of startling duration and effect and later pushed the Rochester fuel-injection system into production for 1957, he gave the now bored-out 283-inch smallblock an output of 283hp, reckoned at the time to be an unattainable ideal ratio of power to capacity. The hotrodders had adopted the smallblock almost immediately it appeared, and Duntov's work – especially that camshaft, which became an almost mandatory performance option – confirmed their choice. By the same token Chevrolet were not slow to adopt the hotrodding performance tricks, and several times their overbores appeared in action long before similar factory capacities became available. In this way capacity gradually went from its original 265ci through 283ci to 327ci and finally 350ci.

Above: The classic (and collectable) 1963 split-window coupe.

Left: A 1955 Convertible. The enlarged and gold-colored 'V' in the Corvette script reveals a V8 model.

Right: Finished in Polo White, like the Motorama car, the 1955 models were the last with the original shape retained from 1953.

This engine went on to become the most widely produced powerplant ever, and more than 35,000,000 have since been made. Since its introduction in 1955 the V8 has become standardized at 350ci and standard as the GM powerplant for passenger vehicles, gradually being replaced by the 229 V6 during the early to mid-1980s. Although the V6 features across the GM range – including the GTP Corvette race car – the V8 remains the preferred powerplant for the production Corvette, at least until 1990.

Despite Duntov's best efforts – his first task had been to give Corvette some proper suspension and steering geometry, improving its handling almost beyond recognition – things could hardly be described as satisfactory during its early years. GM production philosophy was not, in the 1950s or since, geared to low-volume specialist vehicles, and had not Ford produced the Thunderbird two-seater when they did then Corvette may never have made it past 1955. Later on in life it came under attack from all sides, most notably from Shelby's astounding Cobras and then his Mustangs, even eventually facing in-house competition from Camaro, Firebird and latterly Fiero.

The fact that it survived all these crises was largely down to the fierce loyalty of those who worked on the program and struggled hard to give it the equipment and performance it needed, despite the stringent hand of the GM cost-accounting system. Even the Corvette's independent rear suspension was bought by compromise. The transverse leaf spring was part and parcel of careful budgeting, as were the front suspension components, stolen straight from the existing Chevrolet lines. The introduction of disk

Above: Silver anniversary year in 1978 saw the introduction of the glassback models.

Above right: In 1984 the shape changed completely for the first time since 1968. A specification and price rise took Corvette into the supercar league.

Left: The muscle shape. A 1969 sidepipe model. The chrome-bumper cars are becoming more and more valuable.

Below: The 1978 cars bore commemorative badgework.

UNLEADED FUEL ONLY

brakes was delayed more as a result of perfectionism than accounting, though, and a whole generation of Corvette owners is now familiar with the incredible straight-line stopping power of its massive four-wheel disks.

One of the few people who gave Corvette sound backing at boardroom level (outside of those initially concerned with its creation) came from the unlikely direction of the energetic and enigmatic John De Lorean, whose job at Chevrolet, cloaked under the heading of 'rationalization' was to set the giant among GM divisions back on the trail to profit. De Lorean employed the tactics he had learned at Pontiac to turn the production line and quality control on its head at the same time as he upped the sticker price to make low-volume production more reasonable financially. Part of this program meant the delaying of production-line changes which were in hand, and partly accounts for the fact that Corvette retained a virtually unchanged body style for 15 years.

Although it was an eye-catching and attractive style, 15 years is an exceptionally long time in the auto industry. At Corvette the absence of change was by no means due to a lack of ideas or enthusiasm. During this lengthy period many of the most exciting Corvette development prototypes were built, including a variety of mid-engine cars, several of which refected GM's fairly long but ultimately unsuccessful flirtation with the Wankel rotary.

What happened instead was that the superb styling work which went on under the leadership of the visionary Bill Mitchell went into production without the engineering changes which people like Duntov believed to be central to a car like Corvette. Best-known of these was the Mako Shark show car, which went into production as the 1968 Sting Ray when the mid-engine layout had been dropped as a result of the tooling costs involved in creating its transaxle. All the really advanced work which had been going on behind the scenes was relegated to the purely experimental. Although Corvette engineering was somewhat retarded by all this, it was far from being bad. While most Detroit option boxes were concerned with cosmetic items, those for Corvette were almost exclusively concerned with engineering parts – final drive ratios, spring rates and engine parts. This was totally in keeping with the original Corvette ethos, and underlined a basic truth – it was a very good-looking car.

Corvette's longest-awaited restyle finally made the streets in 1984 (there was no 1983, 30-year anniversary model) after lengthy development work by Jerry Palmer (styling) and Dave McLellan (Chief Engineer). Incorporating a wind-cheating body, a hi-tech reworked 350 V8 and $25,000 sticker price, it put Corvette firmly into the supercar league. Further engine work gave 1985 models a 150mph capacity again, the first time for almost 20 years. Extra electronic development work, which raises the compression ratio and improves engine management, means that the 170mph Corvette could be with us again very soon.

57 CHEVY

Every once in a while you get a car or a project which, for no discernible reason, everything goes wrong. The Edsel is a classic example. And every so often you get a car in which, for no noticeable reason, everything goes absolutely right all the way down the line. The 57 Chevy is a classic example – and a classic.

Chevrolet styling had become somewhat slabby and behind-hand by the early 1950s, and a serious restyle was definitely called for. The 1953 facelift was applied to all GM cars and laid the groundwork for what was ahead. Chevrolet broke much new ground in 1955 and it was a crucial year for GM.

Most works on classic cars concentrate on styling, on graceful curbside elegance and long, flowing lines. But in 1955 Ed Cole produced the direct engineering equivalent. The smallblock V8 was an industry milestone, destined to become the most successful auto engine in history, destined to be exactly the right product for sedans, sportscars, vans and race cars. Its impact was so great that it is impossible to separate it from the story of the Tri-Chevys, the classic styling pieces from 1955, 1956 and 1957.

Ford had ruled the performance roost for decades. The flathead V8 had been around since the Model B of 1932 and was *the* performance option. Chevrolet had not made a V8 engine for decades, and even the 1953 facelift cars still relied on the faithful but turgid 'stovebolt' six.

Then along came the Ed Cole smallblock. It came from the drawing-boards of Cole and Harry Barr, and it was designed on a clean-sheet 'perfect world' basis. Because of this, because Cole and Barr were so certain that a good engine simply had to include certain dimensions and relationships and because, as Cole explained later, they *knew* they had got it right, the engine was released for tooling direct from their drawing-boards.

With a displacement of 265ci, it weighed in at less than the old straight six but packed a 180hp punch with a four-barrel carburetor. The special relationship between bore and stroke allowed it to rev freely to limits which would put contemporary production V8 engines into the nearest trashcan. It was a gem, and 30 years later its reputation is still so strong that it is the biggest obstacle to its successful replacement.

It was with the Powerglides, in conjunction with this engine, that GM first began to acquire their reputation for excellent automatic transmission; smooth imperceptible shifts with such reliability that they were good enough to be fitted as original equipment to Rolls-Royce.

Above and left: GM publicity shots for the most elegant of the classic Chevys, the 57 Bel Air.

Right: Beyond doubt one of the best-looking GM cars of all time, the 1957 two-door Bel Air.

All pictures: The top of the range; the 1957 Bel Air convertible had everything going for it – good looks and a fuel-injected V8 – but sold less well than the 1955 and 1956 models.

What made the mid-1950s Chevrolets really great was, of course, their styling. This was still the era of Harley Earl, and the tailfin, the wraparound windshield and a little chrome-plated flamboyance were still essential ingredients of the auto styling studios. Under Earl's rule the Chevrolet team of Clare MacKichan, Chuck Stebbins, Bob Veryzer and Carl Renner produced the first really up-to-date designs GM had managed during the decade. There were elements of the Autorama dream cars from Cadillac, Oldsmobile and Buick included, and Carl Renner turned the Corvette-based Nomad station wagon dream car from 1954 into a 1955 Bel Air station wagon which gained more than respectable sales. Even so the three-year total of only 22,375 makes the Nomad a desirable collector's item.

Overall the 1955 cars reached a 1,700,000 production run, and the range made over 4,000,000 during their three-year lifespan. In 1956 they reached a record 28 percent penetration with a similar production level, but 1957, with the most elegant cars, was the smallest production year. There had been a facelift in 1956, but it had been very slight, retaining most of the hallmarks of the previous model. One thing which had changed was the egg-crate grille. Unpopular with the customer, it had reputedly been one of Harley Earl's favorite touches, but out it went.

The year 1957 saw some much deeper changes to the styling, and it was without doubt this year's model which was the most elegant of the three. The major elements of the original 1955 cars had been retained, but around the dipped beltline was a new,

lighter elegance – despite the extra chrome which now surrounded a wraparound oval grille which evoked memories of Ferrari's Superamerica. This was the era of unnecessary chromework and while other GM cars got theirs in different years (Corvette in 1958, Cadillac in 1959) this was Chevrolet's year.

Launched in the October of 1956, there were no less than 19 models from the basic 150 2-doors right up to the top-of-the-range Bel Air convertibles (in fact the Nomad was more expensive, but hardly top-of-the-range). Despite the excellence of these cars they fared less well than the 1955 and 1956 models in the marketplace. That was largely because both Ford and Plymouth produced a major restyle for 1957, although in retrospect the 1957 Fairlanes look similar to the 57 Chevy, only clumsier. But the Plymouth success story was in its ascendancy at the time, and Virgil Exner's designs for 56 and 57 were announced as 'The Forward Look', allowing the Plymouth agency to claim 'suddenly it's 1960.' Despite Exner's indisputable abilities, the Plymouths too now look rather awkward compared to the Chevrolet offerings.

The Chevys had another big advantage for 1957 too, as they got new versions of Ed Cole's V8. This included the fuel-injected 283 which had been rush-developed because Duntov badly wanted it for the 1957 Corvette. It packed 283hp, one for each cubic inch of capacity – another industry milestone – and it made the 57 cars formidable pieces of racing equipment. Even the big Bel Air turned in 17-second quarters and topped out at over 110mph; the two-door 150 was both lighter and faster.

In fact 1957 was shaping up to be quite a successful competition year, with some good NASCAR showings and some even better results at the Daytona Speed Week. In one class they took 33 out of 37 places. But 1957 was the year the AMA announced their no-race policy and all that involvement went out of the window. The facelift cars for 1958 were bigger in every dimension except performance, with softer suspension and bigger carrying capacity. There was no chance that these later cars like the Biscayne and the Impala could show the economy of line of their predecessors, even though Chevrolet stylists were the first to go against the tailfin styling trend in 1958. (Although they came back with a vengeance on the 1959 Biscayne and Impala.)

For that brief three-year span between 1955 and 1957, Chevrolet offered vehicles which were destined to become classics, destined to become collectors' items and destined to become a street-rodder's favorite. The more brutal 1955 cars took their place in movie history; Harrison Ford's 1955 from *American Graffiti* became James Taylor's 1955 in *Two-lane Blacktop* and later still the 57 Chevy became one of only a few cars to be immortalized in its own song.

Above: A 1957 Bel Air four-door sedan, one of 19 choices in the range.

Above right: The pillarless two-door had sleeker lines than the family sedan.

Right: Even the station wagon was good-looking. The Bel Air Nomad was, obviously, the top luxury wagon in the range.

EDSEL

Henry Ford's son, Edsel was the man responsible for the creation of the original Lincoln Continental. When Henry gave Edsel control of the new division (after he had bought it from beneath Henry Leland at the end of World War I) Edsel immediately declared his intention of making the Lincoln name synonymous with excellence. His father made the most popular car in the world, he was going to make the best.

Although it is possible to split hairs, there is no doubt that the Lincoln name is associated with quality, with luxury, with prestige and even with Presidents. It is ironic, then, that Edsel's name should not only be linked with one of America's ultimate prestige vehicles but also with one of its all-time turkeys.

To be fair, though, the turkey had nothing to do with Edsel, except that it bore his name. He took over control of the Ford Motor Company after his father's retirement in 1941, but Edsel himself died in 1943. Henry Ford moved back into power but

control passed next to Edsel's son, Henry Ford II. It was under his rule, in the mid-1950s, that the great American turkey appeared. This was not the Ford Edsel but a separate manufacturing division of the Ford Motor Company which produced Edsel Rangers, Edsel Pacers, Edsel Corsairs and even Edsel Citations.

The need for this separate division became apparent to Ford in the mid-1950s. It was the dawn of the medium-size automobile, a type of car which had been gaining tremendous popularity. However it was a somewhat brief affair, and almost immediately the sales charts began to show signs of decline. By the time the Edsel appeared it was almost too late, and its tardy appearance not only sealed its fate but also gave rise to the most famous of its numerous epitaphs: 'Its aim was right, but the target moved.'

The GM divisions had more or less created the need for this size of car and all had a medium-sized, medium-priced product. Pontiac and Buick were rivalled only by Dodge, and by 1955 had

boosted this new market to around 2,000,000 vehicles a year. Clearly it was not something which Ford could afford to ignore or be left out of. They were well placed with smaller, lower-priced cars like their own Fairlane, and were equally well placed higher up the scale with Edsel's old Lincoln division. Mercury was Ford's only weapon in about the right area and price, and in fact the 1955 models were the most popular for years. The line was slowly heading up-market, though, as well as up in size and price, so a completely new division was seen as the best way to attack the medium market.

Development work began in earnest during 1955, with a first year goal of 100,000 units for its debut appearance, scheduled for 1958. There were to be four models in that year. Ranger and Pacer were placed over a 118-inch wheelbase which they shared with that year's Fords, while Corsair and Citation were on the 1958 Mercury's 124 inches. Standard powerplants were a 303hp, 361

Left: There were few visual saving graces, even from behind.

Right: The Ford publicity for the Edsel (this is a 1959 Ranger) could not save it.

Below: The Edsel was a reasonably large car, but demand for that size of vehicle had evaporated before it made the streets.

Overleaf, main picture: Top of the range, the 1958 Edsel Citation convertible Coupe is rare indeed – only 930 were built.

Overleaf, inset: Ford launch publicity for the Edsel. 'Remarkable' was a remarkably well-chosen description.

This is the **EDSEL**

"A remarkable new automobile joins the Ford family of fine cars"

EDSEL

EDSEL
NOW AT YOUR EDSEL DEALER

As appearing in Life Magazine, September 9, 1957

smallblock V8 for the first two and a 345hp, 410 for the bigger cars. With the big-block especially, the Edsels were acceptably quick, even with 'tele-touch' automatic transmission.

In fact there was nothing unusual about the transmission itself, but it was operated by buttons recessed in the steering-wheel hub, just one of the Edsel's many gadgets and devices. Power-assistance or electric operation was a feature of almost every item of equipment on the vehicle, and it also made use of the rotating-drum type of speedometer which saw short-lived novelty success in a handful of different cars over the next 20 years or so.

With all this, the Edsel's pricing was pretty accurate, and it came out below the equivalent Mercury by an appreciable margin every time. But with all that going for it, the Edsel was laboring under three serious handicaps which together would make sure that success was never to be part of its story: timing, styling and that name.

Research for the new name had been lengthy, expensive and largely ignored. The Ford agency – Foote, Cone and Belding – had employed one man, David Wallace, especially to quiz the public for their reaction to over 6000 different names. Traditional Detroit-type suggestions like Ranger, Pacer, Corsair and Citation came out at the top of the list and eventually became model designations within the range. But in the quest for originality Wallace sought the assistance of Brooklyn poetess Marianne Moore. The names she dreamed up received a less than rapturous reception during research; 'Silver Sword,' 'Resilient Bullet,' 'Varsity Stroke,' 'Andante Con Moto,' 'Turcotinga,' 'Mongoose Civique' and 'Utopian Turtletop' were some of her best efforts.

It was the Chairman of the Ford Motor Company who finally made the decision over naming. Ernest Breech did not like any of the names which research showed would be popular, and he definitely did not like any of the names Marianne Moore had suggested. He overrode everybody else who was opposed to the idea – including Henry Ford II himself – and opted to call the new division Edsel.

Few people have claimed credit for designing the Edsel, and no wonder. For many years it has been widely accepted as one of the ugliest automobiles ever made. The 1958 and 1959 long-wheelbase cars are particularly afflicted, and it is rumored that there is no single recorded instance of one having been stolen.

It is a peculiar combination of angles and styles with a visual impact that has only recently begun to be softened by the pas-

Above right: That celebrated frontal aspect – the 1959 Edsel Ranger.

Above: Facia, with column shift.

sage of time; but it burst onto the 1958 automobile scene in no uncertain way. Since then opinions towards it have tended to relax, and it is even regarded with something approaching affection. If nothing else it is instantly recognizable and its story does lend it a certain eccentricity of character which is a basic ingredient of nostalgia. Its rarity, of course, is another contributing factor, and although some purists may recoil slightly at the thought, the Edsel is becoming more and more collectable.

The rarity of the Edsel is well established, but blame for this cannot be laid solely at the door of its stylists. Its first-year goal of 100,000 units was never achieved; it only just managed that in its entire three-year lifespan. The reasons center mainly around market influences which are far removed from the nature of a single vehicle. The medium-sized market began shrinking almost the day that the Edsel stylists first laid pen to paper, and from being a 25 percent segment of the market it had shrunk to 18 percent by the time the car appeared in public for the first time. By then it was 18 percent of a market which was itself falling in volume; 1957 was a slump year for the entire auto industry.

Only slightly over 50,000 were built during its first year of manufacture, split over four sedans and two station wagons. In the following year the range was cut to the short-wheelbase Ranger, a new short-wheelbase Corsair and a station wagon which also rode a 120-inch chassis. Engine choice was increased, though, with the 361 V8 the biggest of the four units on offer, backed up by a 332 and a 292 V8, plus a 223 in-line six.

This offered no real sales advantage, and second-year output for all three variants totalled only 26,563. The following year the range was reduced again, being just the 120-inch Ranger and a station wagon with a choice of three engines: 352 or 292 V8 and the 223 straight-six. But even with a consolidated lineup there was still no profit to be found from an annual production of less than 30,000 cars and the Edsel disappeared for good in the November of its third year.

Total production just crept above the first-year target and finished at 106,000; in that final year alone Ford's 118-inch Fairlane sold 175,000 units, so the mathematics were clear.

The sorriest part of the tale is that the car was given a totally unsuitable name which belonged to a man whose own standards, abilities and achievements deserved better than association with a complete flop.

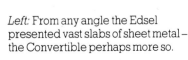

Left: From any angle the Edsel presented vast slabs of sheet metal – the Convertible perhaps more so.

THUNDERBIRD

Ford had dominated the performance areas of the auto market for decades, through the trusty flathead V8. But they had never made anything which could truly be described as a sportscar.

After the war ended the level of handy European two-seaters available in the USA began to increase. Their popularity was in part because of the returning servicemen who had sampled the nimbleness of European chassis design at first hand and were now looking for it at home, bringing the import level up. At the same time as Lord Nuffield gave MG their 'export or die' pep talk, William Lyons gave Jaguar the brand-new XK series and both Ferdinand Porsche and Enzo Ferrari began to build cars in their own name for the first time.

The growing demand for two-seat sportscars was becoming more and more evident and it was largely this which prompted Chevrolet into developing the Corvette in 1953. Ford's two-seat Thunderbird is traditionally seen as a reply to Corvette since it appeared two years later, but it had actually been on the drawing

Bottom left: The 1955 hardtop shows the attraction of clean, simple lines.

Below: From 1955, the elegant Thunderbird two-seat convertible.

Right: The V8 badge on the trunk lid is a clue to Thunderbird's success compared to its rival, Corvette.

All pictures: By 1958 the Thunderbird was no longer a small sportscar, but had been successfully transformed into this very much larger four-seat 'personal car.'

boards since almost the turn of the decade and Corvette was only the spur which pushed the project into sheet-metal.

There are other myths about Thunderbird too. The most common is that it was inspired by the sportscar element of the 1951 Paris Salon and that Lewis Crusoe was the man who carried the good work back to Dearborn. Once again the chronology is out of sync, but clearly this is another contributing factor although it would almost certainly have appeared sooner or later in any case. Ford market research had shown a need for a two-seater and at the time they tended to take much more account of formally gathered information of this kind than GM, as the T-Bird's switch to a bigger format in 1958 demonstrates.

Another clear indication that Ford market research had identified the requirements of the US market more closely than GM was the specification of Thunderbird. When the first Corvettes appeared with slogging straight-six engines and a rather miserable two-speed automatic transmission, they suffered criticism and poor sales. A newcomer two years late, the Thunderbird outsold the Corvette from day one, and it did on a specification which was far higher and which was just what the sporty motorist wanted.

Styling for the Thunderbird came directly from the Ford designers working under Frank Hershey, and right from those early days it brought the Thunderbird out as a big car; on the same 102-inch wheelbase as Corvette, the Thunderbird came out

over 12 inches longer, at 15 feet. Pricewise it was deadly accurate, just $200 more than the Corvette but with a specification sheet which was music to the ears of enthusiasts disappointed with Corvette performance to date. The Thunderbird came in with Ford's 292ci Y-block V8 which gave it 202hp, and a choice of manual (plus overdrive) or automatic transmission.

In this form it survived three years, although the 1957 models were probably the most desirable of all. The 1956 cars had grown a 'continental kit' for spare-tire storage following complaints about lack of trunk space, and it was in this year that the detachable hardtop was given its 'porthole' look by Ford stylist Bill Poyer. Both those were carryovers for 1957, and the small, nondescript tailfins were given a slight extra emphasis. Under the hood there was even better news with the arrival of a 312ci V8 to supplement the 292. A few of these were even offered as 300hp supercharged units.

It all changed in 1958 when information gleaned by the market researchers brought about a major change of philosophy, transforming the Thunderbird from a two-seat sportscar into a four-seat luxury device which Ford called their 'personal car.' This entailed considerable growth, onto a 113-inch wheelbase, and also saw a new unibody construction. Despite its growth (it had ample room for its four passengers) the 1958 model was an attractive, pleasing car to look at and set the tone for the next

three years. Nevertheless the market researchers had once again put their collective fingers on the right button and sales of the 1958 models were almost double that of the previous year.

The 1959 sales were better still and the styling was virtually unchanged for 1960. New standard power came from a 300hp V8 with a capacity of 352ci, and a big-block 430 with some 350hp on tap (from Lincoln's Continental range) was available as an option. It was a popular option too, as was the hardtop; the convertibles were being outsold eight to one, conclusive proof if it was needed that the luxury car decision dictated by the research had been absolutely correct.

The three-year cycle changed again in 1961, and this time Thunderbird got a pointed front end and long, flowing lines of elegant simplicity. Now with only one engine option, of 390ci, sales were down on previous years and would stay down throughout the life of this body style. Ford stressed reliable build quality and excellent ride comfort but these were the most conservative T-Birds yet. Dealers were constantly being asked for another two-seater (and this continual demand would eventually result in the appearance of the Mustang) so Lee Iacocca gave the go-ahead for a two-seat styling exercise which in 1962 and 1963 became the Sports Roadster.

Stylist Bud Kaufmann created a fiberglass tonneau cover which clipped in behind the front seats, contained 'streamliner' headrests for the front passengers and allowed the soft top to be raised and lowered while it was in place. This conversion added $650 to the price of a car which cost less than $5000, making it a rare car. The following year the cover (and the Kelsey-Hayes wire wheels which went with it) were offered as an option.

The Thunderbird entered another three-year styling cycle in 1964, with new sheet metal which still retained the flavor and character of the previous models. The pointed front was squared off into something which recalled the squat 1958 cars, but the overall T-Bird look was maintained with the basic elements of the swept-up chromework surrounding the grille.

Luxury was an ever-stronger element by now, and with this model came 'Silent-Flo' ventilation, disk brakes, sequential turn signals, the practical 'Swing-Away' steering wheel and a power-operated convertible top. Once again the 390ci V8 was the only engine option, and after an initial upsurge in its introductory year sales began to drift downwards. Convertibles were a smaller and smaller element and accounted for less than 8 percent of production in 1966 – their final year.

By now the Mustang had largely taken up the role of Ford's performance flag-waver and the Thunderbird was more and more a large luxury sedan. One popular move had been the introduction of the ersatz convertible, the Landau hardtop, and it was clear that Thunderbird buyers were expecting status and prestige rather than genuine four-seater performance.

The 1967 restyle saw a Thunderbird looking rather like Mercury's 'stretched' Mustang, and by the end of the decade it had become little more than a four-seat sedan with a colorful past.

Right: The facelift for 1961 had changed the T-Bird yet again, and 1962 cars, like the one pictured, were the best sellers yet.

Below: Sleek, sporty lines were still a feature, and the two-seaters, the Sports Roadsters, had molding behind the rear seats. They also had Kelsey-Hayes wire wheels, which make fitting of the rear fender-skirts impossible.

ELDORADO

Founded in 1903 out of the remains of the failed Henry Ford Manufacturing Co by Henry M Leland, the Cadillac company was named after Antoine Cadillac, the founder of Detroit. Leland immediately set about making cars of great excellence, a matter which had been at the root of his disagreements with Ford. While Henry had believed in manufacture by bulk, and had been firmly convinced that the path to success lay through selling volume at low price with a small profit margin, Leland took the opposite point of view.

Leland believed in engineering excellence above all else, and he also believed that car buyers would recognize and pay for it. As it happened, they were both right, and both their business ventures established after the partnership split were destined for success and a place in Detroit mythology.

While Ford went on to set up his mass-production goal, Leland followed a different quest. An engineer by training and by inclination, Leland had worked for the Springfield Armory during the Civil War and then for Samuel Colt. Later he became technical adviser and engine supplier to Ransom E Olds, and then a supplier of engines to Henry Ford's first (failed) enterprise, the Detroit Manufacturing Co. After the ill-fated partnership with Ford, he reorganized the Henry Ford Manufacturing Co as Cadillac.

In later years Alfred P Sloan, the man who made Billy Durant's dream for General Motors come true, said of Leland 'Quality was his God,' something future customers would not only believe but frequently depend on.

The first Cadillac of 1902 was powered by nothing more than a single-cylinder Ford engine, but engineer Leland presided over much in the way of technical advance, and a mere 12 years later his own design V8 engine became the standard Cadillac powerplant. Cadillac's reputation for excellence was quickly established in this short period, and although Ford introduced the auto industry to mass production, Leland was the first to standardize vehicle components to the point at which they were interchangeable. Cadillac was the first Detroit company to make cars fitted with electric lights, and then the first to make pioneering use of the electric starter which had just been perfected by 'Boss' Kettering's Dayton Electric Laboratories (now GM's Delco Division). Leland's confidence in the system was such that Cadillacs from then on made no allowance for the use of a starting handle whatsoever, although other makers still supplied them 50 years later.

By now Cadillac was beginning to rival Packard as the most prestigious American automobile manufacturer, but its reputation had been built on more than straightforward technical advance; it was Leland's wholehearted pursuit of quality which had contri-

buted the most. Cadillac's quality could be proved; in 1911 Cadillac won the Dewar Trophy. This prestigious award was made after two Cadillacs had been reduced to their component parts and those parts had been thoroughly intermingled. Two cars were then successfully rebuilt from the box of mixed parts, proving that their manufacturing tolerances were to such high standard that parts were indeed interchangeable – not something which could be said of other vehicles of the time.

After that Cadillac went from strength to strength, eventually being incorporated into the acquisitive Billy Durant's growing General Motors empire. Leland went off to form Lincoln and soon became involved in manufacturing materiel for the US effort in World War I; even without him Cadillac's reputation soon established it as the GM flagship and the transport of Presidents. By strange irony Lincoln fell into Henry Ford's hands and he, perhaps irate that the remainder of his old venture had passed on to his GM rival as Cadillac, soon removed Leland from control of Lincoln. Even more ironic is that under Edsel's guidance Lincoln became the Ford flagship, so ensuring that both of Leland's companies were rivals at the very top of the auto market.

As makers of exclusive and expensive cars, Cadillac survived both the Depression and the war thanks to the solidity of the GM combine, while firms like Packard slid further and further into recession until they closed. During the 1930s Cadillac produced one of the great American automobiles of all time, the V16. As a

Above: The most ostentatious car ever made? The dizzy heights of Harley Earl's aviation imagery in glass, chrome and rear tailfin, the 1959 Cadillac Eldorado Biarritz Convertible.

Right: The facia of the 59 models was almost restrained by comparison to the outside.

Sedan de Ville it was an impressive status symbol, while as a rather rakish Cabriolet it rivalled anything produced by the ACD combine or any of the overtly sporty-car makers in Europe.

In fact the V16 Sedan de Ville is frequently described as one of the greatest American cars of all time. At 148 inches, the chassis was nothing if not luxurious, and the rest of the car followed the same theme. Coachwork was by Fleetwood, whose work was by now exclusive to Cadillac, and made the most of the flowing grace of the fenders to compensate for what was of necessity a large and squarish body behind a vast, imposing grille. Behind it, Ernest Seaholm's 45-degree 454 V16 engine was one of Detroit's better efforts, producing a quiet, smooth 165hp at only 3400rpm. Introduced in 1931, the V16 lasted to 1940, during which time 4435 were built.

Postwar Cadillacs were still built to the same high standard – their slogan had been 'Standard of the World' since the days of Henry Leland and the Dewar Trophy – and were, incredibly, still built on almost the same scale. The Series 75 grew from 136 inches in 1945 to 146 in 1950 and 149 inches in 1954, but that was the standard Cadillac 9-passenger stretchout for state occasions.

The Series 70 Eldorado Brougham, introduced in 1957, began life on a modest 126-inch chassis but in 1959 became the Cadillac Eldorado in three forms: the Seville Hardtop Coupe; the Brougham Hardtop Sedan; and the Biarritz Convertible Coupe. All versions rode a 130-inch chassis.

Cadillac later said that the 1959 Eldorado was the most ostentatious car they ever made, and while that may be true it is still not completely accurate: the 1959 Cadillac Eldorado was the most ostentatious car anybody ever made.

The use of tailfins had been largely the work of Harley Earl, head of GM styling until 1958. His second love, after the automobile, was aircraft, and it was the legendary Misterearl who had adopted the wraparound screen and stubby wings of contemporary jet fighters to his mid-1950s cars. Nowhere was this more evident than in Cadillac's 'Cyclone' dream car from 1959. With a lift-off perspex bubble roof, the body had two pointed 'booms,' one down each side, projecting clear of the bodywork at front and rear. Massive pointed wings rose vertically clear of the rear deck, and the Cyclone looked exactly like a grounded jet plane.

This was a period of styling excess in all areas, not just auto-

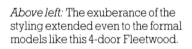

Above left: The exuberance of the styling extended even to the formal models like this 4-door Fleetwood.

Above right: The front aspect was imposing to say the least and, like everything else on the car, was twice as ostentatious as it ought to have been.

Right: It was the rear which was overdone, with mock grille and those huge light-bearing fins.

mobiles, and as the tailfins were accepted as an essential part of design they were taken to greater and greater excess. In 1959, reflecting the Cyclone dream car, Cadillac took the feature to what would be its absolute production limit. As the first models for the new decade appeared the whole thing began to die away again.

The 1959 Eldorado, though, had tail fins large enough to grant in-flight stability to anything so far launched from Cape Canaveral. They were little short of ridiculous in size, soaring from a rear deck which was itself of impressive proportions.

The front was no less dominating, the hood itself was a vast area of sheet steel flowing into quad headlamps and a rambling honeycomb grille, itself dominated by a huge chrome bumper. It also featured the high-output version of the standard Cadillac 390ci V8 motor, putting out 345hp instead of 325hp.

Other standard equipment on the Eldorado was available throughout the whole Cadillac range, and makes impressive reading even now. Self-levelling air suspension (which was not 100 percent successful), cruise control and even signal-seeking radios were also fitted.

The Eldorado was priced according to its immense size and specification. At a time when Lincoln had nothing over $6000 and Chevrolet's typical prices were less than $3000, the Eldorado range began at $7401, only exceeded by the $10,000 for the larger Series 75. But not even the big limo could match the Eldorado Brougham for price – a staggering $13,075. The high price was entirely due to the fact that for 1959 production of this model had been handed over to Pininfarina; the parts were shipped and assembled in Italy and whole cars were sent back. Because of the way it was done the cost was astronomical, and a mere 99 of them were built in 1959, and 101 the following year.

Despite their cost, and although hindsight has lent the whole range an elegance and grace which was perhaps not completely evident at the time, the Biarritz Convertible is the most impressive of the three Eldorados; it is the stuff of movies and television, it is the huge pink car featured in just about every cartoon series of the late 1950s and early 1960s, it is the sort of car movie moguls gave to starlets and genuine screen goddesses gave to their friends at Christmas. Paul Getty owned a 1959 Eldorado, but his was the Seville hardtop; at no time was the Biarritz a car to be taken seriously.

Left: The rambling chrome grille of the 1959 Eldorado.

Below: This was the ultimate expression of the late 1950s tailfin craze – even one light would have been an overstatement.

Below right: The front view was almost as ostentatious as the rear, and also featured the 'dual' theme, with twice as many lights, twice as many grille teeth and twice as much chrome as necessary.

Above right: From ground level the true breathtaking scope of the fins and the vast amount of sheetmetal becomes apparent.

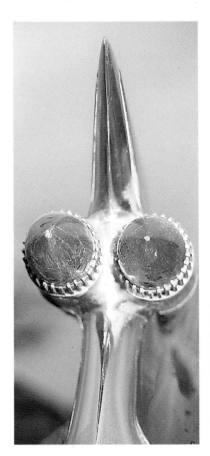

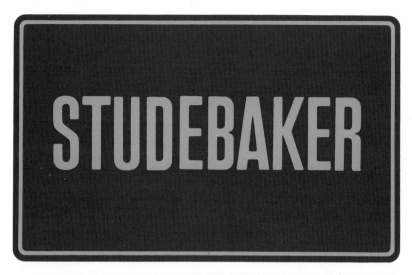

STUDEBAKER

The Studebaker Corporation can claim to have been involved in the transportation industry longer than any other American manufacturer, with a history of building horse-drawn wagons which goes right back to 1852. In 1902 it switched to making automobiles and almost immediately hit trouble.

Studebaker had managed quite well for around 20 years but as the industry generally began to hit some lean years the Studebaker low-price contender, the Erskine, missed its market by a mile and brought serious financial difficulties. This unhappy plight was compounded by the 1929 crash, and that was followed by the unfortunate Rockne, introduced in 1931 and named after a football coach. It flopped gradually, lowering the company into receivership by 1933.

Rescue came in the form of Paul Hoffman and Harold Vance; their rebuilding program took the best part of five years. With streamlined administration and management and a range of new products allied to a revitalized dealer network, Studebaker was back on its feet by 1939. The car which put the seal on their recovery was the aptly-named Champion, an economical goodlooker which came from the drawing-board of the man responsible for Aga cookers, Coldspot refrigerators and the *Pittsburgh Flyer*. Born in Paris in 1893, Raymond Loewy had moved into the auto industry via the 1934 Hupmobile and was about to become the pillar of Studebaker postwar success with a series of revolutionary designs which were ahead of their time and frequently scorned.

There were three offerings for 1940, but it was the good-looking Champion which saved Studebaker, putting production above 100,000 units for the first time since 1928. Riding a 110-inch wheelbase, with Studebaker's 'Planar' independent front suspension, it had an L-head straight six with a 164ci swept volume and the highest rev range the industry had yet seen. Small, light and gutsy, it was economical before gas mileage was crucial, yet its frugality (between 10 and 20 percent better than the other budget cars, Ford, Chevrolet or Plymouth) was a strong selling point on which Studebaker was not slow to capitalize.

Facelifts for the 1941 models showed Loewy just beginning to exercise his talents. He showed the first two-toning the industry had ever seen, and sales for the year made Studebaker number eight in the industry – a considerable achievement in less than ten years. The progress was maintained the following year, and by the time civilian vehicle production was halted to make way for military hardware Studebaker had already moved more than 50,000 cars off the South Bend production lines. For the next few years there were no advances in auto design or styling, and although the war years brought terrific technological advance generally, it could not be taken advantage of immediately; the major manufacturers went back into production with whatever they had been building in 1942 when the plants shut down.

Although their very first postwar offerings were facelifted 1942 Champions, Studebaker was able to be different. Loewy had never been part of the company, but had worked on contract. While Detroit design studios had been on skeleton staff – and those occupied on more bellicose projects – Loewy had been

Left: A 1906 Studebaker Model G Tourer, on sale after only four years in the auto industry.

Top right: The 1929 Commander Six Convertible Cabriolet – a high point just ahead of disaster.

Right: The 1949 Champion, one of the advanced Loewy designs, years ahead of rivals with features like its flow-through fenders.

able to give considerable thought to what would happen when the war ended. Among the team he had working in this area was the young Virgil Exner, and although he had split from Loewy before the 1947 cars made production, his influence was considerable. His front-end treatment was preferred over Loewy's and it was Exner's flat front and wide chrome grille which the 1946 cars wore.

Perhaps it was this which spurred Loewy on to greater things, and certainly the 1951 model year saw the arrival of his 'bullet-nose' look, although it was by no means a major change. The fact was that the postwar Studebakers hardly changed at all in their first five years, mainly because the combination of Loewy and Exner had produced designs which were years ahead of their time, and certainly years ahead of Detroit.

But as the Studebaker Corporation reached its centenary year things were once again shaping up badly for them. This must have been hard to believe at the time; 1950 had been their best year ever, but there were forces at work both inside and outside the company which together would once again bring it to its knees. Tucked away in Indiana, removed from the center of the industry – especially vital component suppliers – with an old and now out-dated plant, their overheads were high. Their workers were among the highest-paid in the industry but productivity was unmanageably low. Worse still, and almost certainly the deciding factor, they were caught in the crossfire as Ford and Chevrolet battled for the number-one spot with a series of lengthy and ferocious price wars which irreparably damaged a number of small independent companies.

The merger with Packard may have seemed like a good idea, but basically it saw only the joining of two already crippled companies into one larger organization, which was doubly un-wieldy and unprofitable. Eventually Curtiss-Wright stepped in to add financial muscle and they allowed Packard to fail while Studebaker continued to limp along. The reason is simple

enough: Studebaker product was better, more innovative and generally showed features adopted by the rest of the industry within a couple of seasons.

Studebaker made their first V8 in 1951, and it was a smallblock 232 that stepped boldly away from traditional molds. More efficient than the straight sixes and eights, more compact and acceptable than the flathead V8 and V12, it crossed a barrier for the first time, allowing luxury-car performance at close to economy prices. It would be followed by similar offerings from every major manufacturer.

Then in 1953 came a new range of elegant Studebaker cars which have since become known as the 'Loewy coupes' although they came from the chief of the Loewy South Bend studio, Robert Bourke. They were graceful from any angle, called the 'new European look,' and frequently are held to be the best design work of the decade to come from North America. Although they were an indisputable success the changeover to the new cars took too long and production was lost.

It did not pick up over the next couple of years. At a time when

Above: The new cars from 1953 onward were among the best design work of the decade. This is a 1954 Commander.

Left: At $3061 the Golden Hawk was the top of the range model.

Right: The range was called the 'new European look' or the 'Loewy coupes,' and the Golden Hawk Hardtop Coupe (from 1956) is a fine example.

Left: The Golden Hawk also took the top engine option, a 275hp, 352ci smallblock V8.

Below: The Studebaker Avanti, last model built before the factory closed in 1966. This one dates from 1964; later cars, powered by GM engines, were built by two Studebaker dealers.

any GM plant could have built the Studebaker cars for at least $500 less than South Bend, at a time when the accountants calculated that they needed at least 250,000 sales to break even, production was down to just 116,000 cars. Struggling against overwhelming odds, helpless as the Ford/GM price war hotted up again, Studebaker introduced new models for 1956, the last which Loewy did for them, and probably the best.

The Hawk range was elegantly sporty, with a lean appearance very much in the classic mold but still highly individual. There was a whole range to choose from, including the Packard-powered Golden Hawk, and they were well priced – the Golden Hawk sold for less than the Corvette. But that was no recommendation: Corvette's specialist sales were hardly enough to keep the production lines rolling and had it not been for Thunderbird, the Dearborn two-seat competitor, the Corvette itself would probably have been axed that year.

While the sports coupes held their appeal, overall Studebaker sales continued to fall and the end was clearly in sight. By 1958 it appeared to have arrived. Silver Hawk sold 7000, Golden Hawk a

mere 878. Then stylist Duncan McRae combined a selection of bits from previous models with some new panels and produced a new compact with the unlikely name of Lark. It had an immediate and dramatic effect, almost trebling production in 1959, and the Lark continued to be the mainstay of the company over the next few years.

Loewy was called back to design another sports coupe and the excellent Avanti was the result. It was rushed through every stage of design and preproduction but Loewy's team had done a splendid job; advance orders gave it a very healthy-looking future. Problems with its fiberglass body delayed its introduction and slowed the build rate considerably. By the time the factory could have been up to full rate most of their potential buyers had moved on to Corvette.

Studebaker sales began another gradual decline, so that by 1965 they were down to only 19,435 units. 1966 was their last year, and saw a mere 8947 vehicles. The only survivor was Loewy's Avanti, which continued in production thanks to two South Bend Studebaker dealers, who carried on, using a Corvette engine.

1963 GM issued their stern 'no race' edict, giving the entire company orders to ship out all performance parts within 14 days, just like that.

It left Pontiac high and dry, with nothing to back up their previous barnstorming success. Unable to get near a race track and not allowed to use race success in advertising, Pontiac had to find a new angle. Advertising man Jim Wangers and the magnetic John Z De Lorean went to Pontiac chief engineer Peter Estes with a plan to put the big 389 V8 into the Tempest, a four-cylinder compact which was the smallest vehicle in the range. This was a hotrodders' technique which had slowly been absorbed into legitimate drag racing, the fastest-growing form of motorsport in the USA, but it had never been attempted by a manufacturer before.

The result was the GTO; not a new car in any sense of the word, but simply a selection of options available on the Tempest. In fact it was launched as the Tempest GTO, in much the same way as the Z-28 option on Camaro later became a vehicle designation. Later GTO packages were available on the Le Mans and Catalina, but the GTO was never a car in its own right. The 389 engine which formed the basis of the GTO package was option three hundred and twenty-something, and some buyers did not even see it at the

There can be no doubt at all that the 1960s was a very special decade. The events, the music, the atmosphere, all are difficult to explain to anyone who did not live through it all. To the auto world as well, the 1960s had a special flavor, largely created by that most unlikely of creatures, the musclecar.

The search for horsepower had really begun to move with the arrival of Chrysler's 331 smallblock hemi in 1951. The hemi (hemispherical cylinder head) provides a number of advantages through increased volumetric and thermal efficiency, which translate on to the road as raw power. With only minor modifications the hemi was good for around 350hp, and properly sorted it gave drag racers 1000hp. It appeared at Indianapolis in 1953, giving 400bhp, and stock hemi engines in the Chrysler 300 dominated the 1955 and 1956 NASCAR circuits. The arrival of the fuel-injected 283 Chevy smallblock produced the engineer's goal of 1hp per ci of capacity, and the story would have gone on longer but for the 1957 AMA resolution to 'de-emphasize' racing.

Hit by the decision to back out of racing were GM's Pontiac division. With falling sales and possible closure looming in the future, Pontiac had been handed over to Semon 'Bunkie' Knudsen (son of one of GM's mid-term legends, 'Big Bill' Knudsen) in 1956. His mission to rescue the company began with a market-research program which revealed that Pontiac had no discernible image in the marketplace at all. Typically, Knudsen saw this as an advantage, since it gave him a 'blank sheet' on which to select and project whatever image he chose.

Following this came one of the most far-sighted marketing decisions made in Detroit during the decade. Knudsen saw and recognized the sheer numbers of the rapidly growing youth market and went straight for it. Not only did Pontiac have no image in the marketplace, but these youngsters (many of whom were not yet old enough to hold a driving license) had no image of the market, allowing Pontiac to select any image they chose without offending any existing loyalties.

Using the new 1955 V8, Knudsen went all-out for glossy up-front performance, producing 130mph stormers with 300bhp under the bonnet. Pontiac entered NASCAR, won at Daytona in 1957, 1958 and 1959, tacitly ignoring the AMA ban on motorsport. With the new 'Super Duty' version of the V8 they were practically unbeatable on the dragstrip. Pontiac backed up its sport involvement with a bewildering catalog of performance parts available from the factory, creating performance packages which could be fitted through the dealership program without affecting warranty, and rose from number six to number three in the new car sales league.

Along the way they unwittingly wrote the blueprint for the car that was to be typical of the whole muscle era, created from a family sedan out of the option boxes on the order blank. Then in

Right: The 1965 Pontiac GTO, originally not even a car in its own right, just a factory option on the Tempest.

Below: Called 'the Goat' or 'the Great One,' the 1964 GTO was the car which started the musclecar ball rolling.

If you think Wide-Tracking is just a slogan, you've never been behind the wheel of The Great One.

Slogans don't straighten curves. Or conquer hills with the ease of an Alpine tram. But then, not many cars do, either. Which is why our GTO is so reverently referred to as The Great One. Its ability in the aforementioned situations stems from a standard 400-cubic-inch, 4-barrel V-8. A 3-speed with Hurst shifter. And Fastrak, redline tires that adhere to the road like glue clings to your fingers.

However, The Great One didn't merit *Motor Trend* magazine's

"Car of the Year" accolade merely for its driving prowess. Its polished sheet metal is molded into the shape of tomorrow. And up front, the world's most fantastic bumper. So fantastic, you have to kick it to believe it.

So when you next read that Wide-Tracking in a GTO is great, don't shrug and turn the page. See your Pontiac dealer. Where test drives speak louder than words.

Great American sports also dig Le Mans, Firebird, Catalina, Bonneville and Grand Prix.   Pontiac Motor Division

Wide-Track 1968 Pontiacs

We hate to call Wide-Tracking great. But no one has come up with a better word.

If you choose a '68 GTO for the sport of Wide-Tracking, you'll enjoy everything a 400-cubic-inch, 4-barrel V-8 has to offer. And if you're the kind who has the gift of grab, you'll want to order a 4-speed stick shift. You can also order disappearing headlights, hood-mounted tach and our Ram Air engine (that includes functional hood scoops). Just say the word.

Of course, the '68 GTO is more than a great driving experience. As you can see below, it's all new from the exclusive Fastrak redlines up. Its Wide-Track is wider. Our famous disappearing wipers are standard. And up front,

the most unusual bumper, since bumpers were invented. This revolutionary super-snout is the same color as the car, but won't chip, fade or corrode.

One more thing. All '68 Pontiacs are equipped with a host of new safety features. Things like front and rear body side marker lights, energy absorbing front and rear armrests and padded front and intermediate seatback tops and lower structure.

Now that we've given you an insight to the greatness of Wide-Tracking, where do you go from here? To your Pontiac dealer's, of course.

You can also enjoy America's fastest growing sport in our other fantastic '68 Pontiacs. Including LeMans, Tempest Custom and Tempest.   Pontiac Motor Division

MARK OF EXCELLENCE

Wide-Track 1968 Pontiacs

Above, left and right: The 1966 GTO. Still a Tempest option, it came in three types, including a Convertible, with a 389 V8 of 333 or 360hp.

Previous pages: In 1968 the wide-track Pontiacs appeared. The GTO was given an 'Endura' plastic nosecone and a 400-cubic-inch V8 plus four-barrel carburetor.

bottom of the order blank. This lack of basic design for such a powerful car would be the source of criticism for the entire muscle breed in later years, but it was the GTO which wrote the ground rules.

However, at first the GTO was developed in virtual secrecy; there were strict rules about the power-to-weight ratio of GM products, which effectively limited the size of engine which could be fitted to any particular model. Slapping the huge V8 into the Tempest broke those rules in a spectacular fashion. So at first it was kept hidden at the back of workshops and tended to late nights or weekends. Estes did not even tell Pontiac what was going on. Because Pontiac's small cars could not be fitted with any engine over 330ci without breaking rules, the GTO was first shown to the board as a 326, with the big 389 as an option. Even then the reaction was violent, and De Lorean later said that the meeting came close to degenerating into a fistfight. In any case the Board assured De Lorean that the car had no future and would never sell.

A compromise had to be reached; word of the GTO had already leaked and dealers were beginning to send in orders. The Board decided to accept a limited build of 5000 units, but in its first year the GTO sold 32,000, making it the most successful first-year model Pontiac had ever introduced. Wangers believed that they could have sold twice that number, and he was proved right the next year when they did exactly that.

Basically the GTO was simply a five-seat sedan with a huge engine, giving it sportscar performance in at least one direction – forwards. Externally it had dummy hood scoops and bore the triangular red white and blue GTO insignia on radiator grille, front fenders, rear quarters, trunk lid and dash panel. Slight stiffening of the suspension went some way to coping with the power the engine could deliver, and that was it.

The GTO built its success on a long list of options which made it possible for any buyer to order a tailor-made car incorporating almost any number of personal specifications, from center console through Hurst floor-shift right up to the three-carburetor Tri-Power manifold pack. This was set up to run only the center carburetor up to speeds of around 100mph. Then, or under hard acceleration, the two outer throats opened, and 12 square inches of bore opened in the top of the manifold and began dragging air and fuel into the engine. The GTO had a 'noticeable' power surge around 3300rpm as it rocketed to its rated output of 348bhp.

Left: The 1969 Tempest GTO Sport Coupe, with Ram Air forced induction – functional hood scoops!

Below left: The 1969 convertible with hood-mounted instruments.

Below: The 1970 GTO, and another last-fling plastic facelift before the muscle era was strangled.

Large numbers of purists took exception to Pontiac's use of the GTO designation, which was drawn straight from sportscar racing; almost alone *Car and Driver* spoke out on Pontiac's behalf, claiming the Motown GTO was every bit as good as the Modena GTO. They even arranged a test between the two cars, but on the day their GTO had only seven cylinders working, so they brought a giant 421ci Catalina into play. They found that the Catalina could outdrag the Ferrari with ease but was less agile and lost out on the circuit. Given stiffer suspension, they reckoned Modena could only beat it with a prototype racing car. Furthermore, loaded with every option including power brakes, metal brake linings and handling package the GTO was still $10,000 cheaper than the Ferrari.

The GTO quickly built up its own myth and became the subject of many pop songs; GM eventually produced their own in answer to a rash of people (like Jan and Dean), jumping on the band-wagon. After that came GTO cologne, cuff-links, tie bar, sports jacket, socks, even shoes specially designed for driving GTOs in. The GTO began to appear on TV programs like *My Three Sons*, but made its biggest hit as the Dean Jeffries special 'Monkee-mobile' which arrived at the height of Monkeemania. Each member of the Monkees was given a GTO for personal use, and PR hype hit an all-time high when Mike Nesmith was stopped on the Hollywood Freeway after clocking 125mph.

Pontiac had created a brand new marketing technique. Although the GTO had set a whole new set of technical standards – it was the first to have the Hurst shifter available as a factory-fitted option – it also set the trends for the way the rest of the musclecar breed was presented, marketed and hyped. The GTO was on the back of cornflake packets, was given away in competitions, was in stores everywhere as a model kit by Monogram, and in its final fling as The Judge, was the star of 'Two-Lane Blacktop.'

Z-28 CAMARO

When Ford entered the sportscar arena in the 1950s with its Thunderbird Corvette competitor, it changed swiftly to a four-seat layout and immediately saw a massive sales increase. It was logical, then, that Ford's 1960 entrant would also be a four-seater. Yet when it came, the Mustang caught the rest of Detroit completely off-balance, and it had a clear two-year lead before the other manufacturers caught up.

Responsibility for the Chevrolet response was given to GM Art and Design, then under the leadership of Bill Mitchell. They produced a design in what was to become the classic ponycar

mold established by Mustang – low roofline, long hood, short deck, flat nose and flat tail. In this form the Camaro went into production for the 1967 model year.

More than just its looks, the Mustang gave Detroit another sales tool – a massively long option list which would also become another classic feature of the ponycar. The Camaro came with 81 different factory options and 41 dealer-installed accessories which allowed buyers to tailor their new car to an exact and individual specification. The Camaro was available in more guises than any other single car in production at the time. The Camaro base engine was a 140hp straight six with a more powerful 155hp version as an option. There were also two V8 choices, the 327 and, exclusive to Camaro in this first year, the new 350 smallblock which would soon become the GM standard powerplant.

There was also a third V8 option available on Camaro. Although officially GM were no longer involved in racing of any sort this had all the hallmarks of a straightforward homologation exercise aimed directly at the Trans-Am series. The new engine just sneaked the Camaro into Group 2, which had a top limit of 305ci. More interestingly FIA rules required a minimum of 1000 cars be generally available, and the 302 engine formed the basis of the Z-28 package which was available at Chevrolet dealers for street use. This was the most performance-oriented Camaro of them all and signified the top Camaro option until the arrival of the IROC-Z in 1985.

An indication of the Z-28 racing status is evident from the sales figures. In its first year almost 75 percent of Camaro's 220,917 sales

Right and below: A 1969 Camaro Z-28. This designation was originally an option number for the hot 302 V8 engine with assorted performance parts, but GM marketing men soon picked up on its possibilities as a sales tool.

Ten years separate the go-for-broke musclecar Z-28 (*top three pictures*) and the overdressed 1981 version (*below*). Body changes were the plastic nose and tail sections, plus wraparound back light. The real difference was under the hood.

MUSTANG

Lee Iacocca had been in the front-line of the Ford sales team when they had converted their two-seat Thunderbird into a four-seat limousine. Despite the undoubted success of this move (sales up from the 15-month 1957 run of 21,380 to a 9-month figure of 35,758 for the four-seater 1958 model) Iacocca could clearly remember the number of people who had pleaded with Ford for the restoration of the indubitably elegant two-seater.

Now, elevated to Ford Presidency, he began to look again at that market and consider a replacement for the two-seat T-bird. In any case he was on the brink of making his famous statement committing Ford as a whole to their Total Performance ethos; he believed firmly in the sales boost which a successful race program could provide and a performance-oriented production car

was central to this marketing strategy. So in 1961 a first prototype was prepared. Its initial parameters were almost identical to those laid down for Corvette ten years earlier; small, fast and relatively inexpensive at $2500, it had projected sales of 100,000 units a year.

The prototype was rather too innovative to qualify on price grounds; it was a mid-engined wedge-shaped fiberglass device on a 90-inch wheelbase. Power came from the V4 motor from the Cardinal, and it was an extremely good-looking car which would not be too far out of place in the 1980s. Iacocca rejected it almost immediately on the grounds that it could never become a volume-production car. More prototypes were looked at in private before Iacocca saw the car he was looking for, and although the Mustang II show car retained many of the styling characteristics of the first prototype it was, unlike its ill-fated predecessor, conventionally laid-out and immediately recognizable as a Mustang to modern eyes.

The eventual production prototype appeared on a conventional 108-inch chassis, had four seats and was powered by a 170ci Falcon straight-six or the small 260 V8. The body was the work of David Ash, Joe Oros and Gayle Halderman of Ford's design studios, and it set the style of what was to be christened the 'ponycar' in Mustang's honor for the next decade, as the rest of Detroit worked hard to catch up. The arrival of the Mustang took the rest of the industry completely by surprise, and as it tapped a previously unknown market area its sales success was nothing less than phenomenal.

There was a choice of body styles; the Mustang came as a hardtop, a convertible or a fastback coupe, styles which would stay with it virtually unchanged for years. It exceeded Iacocca's wildest dreams in its first year of production and became the

Above: The emblem which gave Detroit a brand new market for 'pony cars.'

Right: A 1965 Mustang is wheeled into the photographic studio for its launch publicity shots.

Below: At the time they were the least popular of the three body styles and were built in smaller numbers – which is why early convertibles like this 1966 are now so highly prized.

greatest single automotive success story of the 1960s, selling 680,000 units in the first nine months of production and setting an all-time record for first-year sales of a new model. It was introduced in April and by September the power choice had changed to include either the 120hp 200ci six or the bored-out 289 V8 which delivered 200hp, 225hp or 271hp, but this was just the start of the progression to big horsepower.

The real secret of the Mustang's appeal was hidden in the option boxes on the dealer order blanks. Buyers were able to order a basic compact or a full-house race car via the possible mix of three- or four-speed stick-shifts, handling package, disk brakes, power steering, air conditioning, tachometer, bench or bucket seats, you name it. Naturally there was also a selection of special badgework, stripes and body moldings available on option.

Although convertibles sold well initially (100,000 in 1965) figures fell progressively and in 1970 only 7000 were sold. The fastback did well, at 77,000 in 1965, but the big success was the notchback, which sold 500,000 units in the first year.

Those ratios were reflected in its second year, when once again it had a whole market area to itself. Although the totals were slightly down on 1965, 607,568 was still not a bad number by any standards. Once again it was the notchback (the hardtop coupe, as it was called) which led the way with 499,751 units, the convertible was a poor second with 72,119 and the fastback third with just 35,698. This was the last year that Mustang had the floor to itself; 1967 witnessed the arrivals of competitors from the rest of the industry, including GM's Camaro/Firebird clones.

In 1967, as Mustang sales fell to 472,121, the newly introduced Camaro and Firebird combined hit 303,475 units, split 60/40 in favor of Camaro. There was even a Ford-produced competitor,

Left: A 1967 Fastback Coupe, nowhere near as popular as the Hardtop – what would now be a notchback.

Below far left: A 1969 Mach-1 428 Fastback Coupe with Ram Air.

Below, left and right: Interior and engine from 1970 – the last year of real Mustang muscle.

Left: The 1973 Sportsroof Coupe was big, overweight and underpowered.

Below: Convertibles were still available in 1973, although still less in demand than the hardtops.

Right: Standardized on 351 power, a 1973 Sportsroof Coupe.

although the Mercury Cougar, which made just over 150,000 sales, was a larger, more luxurious, up-market version. Mustang needed a change to revive its image and maintain its head start. The big-block engines, a 335hp 390ci and a 390hp 427, arrived in 1968, although the real performance Mustangs all bore Carroll Shelby's nameplate. Nonetheless they were solid, fast cars providing the musclecar market of the 1960s with a reliable diet of exactly what was required.

Mustang's first big facelift came in 1969 with the Mach 1. It provided a taste of what was in store for the future; it was longer, lower and wider, and gained dummy hood scoops and vents and a rear deck spoiler. Also new to the lineup was the 351 small-block, giving 250hp or 290hp, in the same year that low-compression engines became a reality and the two big-block engines dropped in output, the 390 down to 320hp, the 428 down to 335hp.

The year 1970 saw the arrival of the new Boss Mustangs, and they entered the new decade as the spearhead of Ford's muscle program, alongside the Mach 1. Between them there were six

body styles available, but although the hardtop coupe was still the favorite, sales were well down – just below 200,000. Camaro/Firebird were also down, but at just over 150,000 units not by very much.

The Boss was a flashy-looking version of the Mustang such as might suit a performance flagship. Shelby had turned his last few 1969 Mustangs into 1970 models with the addition of some extra paintwork and closed his operation down. So it was left to the Boss to carry Ford's semi-hemi Cobra-Jet NASCAR engine onto the street. This one upped power once again, giving a big-block Mustang a respectable turn of speed from its 375hp – nearly as good as the 1968 big-block. It was just one of seven engine options available, from the 200-inch, 115hp straight six upwards.

There was little more than a year left for real performance cars, and in late 1970 Ford abandoned most of its Trans-Am, USAC and NASCAR events. Road cars too lost their teeth in the face of growing legislation, and in the end the Mustang went the same way as its predecessor, the Thunderbird.

SHELBY

Forced by a heart condition to retire from a successful racing career, Carroll Shelby turned to the manufacture of race cars. His idea was to combine the best of two worlds, matching nimble European chassis and suspension to an American V8. The body and chassis unit he chose came from the tiny AC company at Thames Ditton, England; it was a folded sheet-metal affair making a very basic open two-seater with a very long hood and a tiny cramped cockpit perched in front of a short, bobbed deck.

Ford was not Shelby's first choice of engine – GM declined his proposition, reckoning that their Corvette was already the car Shelby wanted to build. His proposition arrived at Dearborn at a time when Lee Iacocca was laying the foundations of Total Performance and Ford was looking to produce a sportscar to compete with Corvette – they were already at work on the Mustang.

The prototype was built in a California workshop which Shelby shared with Dean Moon and used Ford's new 221 smallblock V8. Painted a different color each time, the prototype made a number of magazine front covers, and glowing road tests soon had customers standing in line for the sportscar which they thought was already in mass production.

However that was never to be; each car was lovingly handbuilt, something Ford cost accountants never properly appreciated or understood. Improvements to design were incorporated into the build as soon as they were finalized, so there are virtually no two cars the same. As the improvements became known many Cobra owners brought their cars back to have them modified. So although the first 75 Cobras built had a 260-inch bored out version of the 221 V8 engine fitted, when Ford offered the engine as a 289 it was immediately used for the Cobra from then on, and many of the existing owners brought their 260 back for a transplant.

In October 1962 the Cobra got its first official track outing at Riverside, and the red car driven by Billy Krause built up a lead of a mile and a half over the rest of the field before breaking a stub axle. It was an unhappy retirement but the potential of the car had been clearly established. Over the next three years it lived up to

Top: The Shelby GT350 powerplant – 306hp from 289 cubic inches.

Left: The Cobras were purebred race cars – as this 289 clearly shows.

Below: The Mustang emblem.

Right: A GT350 – striping and dress-up was all the rage at the time.

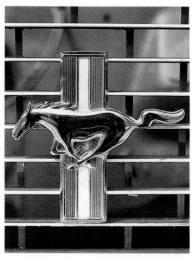

Left: The 1968 GT350 engine.

Right: The badgework was more Ford, less Shelby, although the product was still 'Cobra Tonic.'

Far right: Interior of the 1968 Mustang.

Below: GT500KR (King of the Road). They were made only in 1968, and only 313 convertibles were built.

those expectations completely, and dominated virtually every kind of motor race.

In 1965 the Cobras brought Shelby, Ford and the USA their first ever World Manufacturer's Championship, finally realizing Shelby's dream, which as he expressed it himself, was to 'blow Ferrari's ass off.' To win, the FIA Cobras had done just that at Daytona, Sebring, Oulton Park, Nürburgring, Rossfeld, Rheims and, perhaps sweetest of all, Monza. Le Mans had been the only disappointment; the Cobras ran in second behind Ferrari. The Cobras could probably have won there too, had they used the new 7-liter engines but, apart from sorting the handling with an engine easily capable of giving them a 250mph top speed, Shelby was careful not to offend Ford. Running alongside the Cobras in the 1965 season was the new Ford GT, making its first – none too successful – appearance on the international race circuits. Soon they too would receive Doctor Shelby's 'snakebite' treatment, and the defeat at Le Mans would be more than fully avenged.

Away from international competition the Cobra was also making its name; in drag racing it was so invincible that the rules were changed to keep it out. Privately-owned Cobras were handing out defeat on every oval racetrack in America. In November 1965 Craig Breedlove took a Cobra to Bonneville and grabbed 23 National and International records.

Away from the raceways, the Shelby touch was also being applied to road cars. From 1964 Ford had advertised 'Cobra Tonic,' which was 'Dr Shelby's marvellous elixir for Fairlanes, Falcons and Galaxies, in ten strengths up to 343hp.' Of course there were street-going Cobras, cars which have been the sportscar's touchstone ever since, the performance benchmark by which all are compared. Although such comparisons are somewhat dubious, all other sportscars have been found lacking.

In 1963 Ford introduced the 427 engine and it soon found its way under the Cobra hood, giving a whole new meaning to snakebite. Of the 1011 Cobras Shelby made, 356 were these heart-stopping screamers. The 427, coil-sprung, alloy-bodied Cobras had a performance curve which was almost vertical, with 485hp bringing 60mph in 4.3 seconds from standstill. There were even some versions which could do it in 3.8 seconds. 0-100mph disappeared in 8.6 seconds, and 0-100 and stop took a phenomenal 14 seconds.

Standing quarters took a mere 12.2 seconds, and it had a top speed of 162mph. These sort of figures from a production vehicle are incredible, they are still outstanding on a racetrack or a drag strip, and this car was being built long before Woodstock, before the Apollo moonshot, before LBJ got tough in Vietnam.

The road test reports on the 427 Cobra were enthusiastic:

It's only fair to warn you that out of the 300 guys who switched to the 427 Cobra only two went back to women . . . unless you own real estate near the Bonneville salt flats you'll never see the top end . . . a Cobra is a race car with enough legality built into it so you can drive it on the street . . . the only accessory which comes with the Cobra is a Highway Patrol Car in back of you. Way back . . . I bought the 427 from Shelby on the spot and gave him a check, using my driver's license for identification. We both realized that it might be the last time either of us would see the document.

In 1965, with the FIA GT Championship under his belt, Shelby withdrew the Cobras from competition, and they were succeeded on the track by the Ford GT. However the 'mobile test-bed' GT project produced little in the way of results until it was passed over to Shelby; with that loving touch that Ford had still not recognized or understood Shelby gave it the help it needed and it immediately, and repeatedly, fulfilled the Shelby dream again. In the process it gave Ford the international success it needed and left Ferrari in its dust as the GT40 won the 24 Heures du Mans with a 1-2-3 procession in 1966, and further victories in 67, 68 and 69.

At the same time as Shelby withdrew the Cobras from racing, the latest hot Mustang made its debut. Ford strongly believed in Total Performance as a sales tool. 'Race on Sunday, sell on Monday' was the slogan of the day. It was logical, then, that the snakebite treatment should be applied to Ford's new Corvette-basher, the Mustang, and the first sign of it was the Shelby GT350. This should not, however be confused with any other kind of Mustang. Like the Cobra it was a car designed for racing – there were no compromises from Shelby. Like the Cobra it was built on an individual basis and practically all of the 562s produced in the inaugural year of 1965 were different. Modifications and improve-ments were again added as they were finalized, and if the line ran short of a part, a trim item or a color then the cars were built without that part.

In Shelby trim the Mustangs were superb, but made Ford no real profit. After 250 or so had been built Dearborn accountants made a few production-line changes which Shelby did not like, but they did improve the appeal of the car. Hertz bought a large number to rent out; the GT350H was available to members of the Hertz Sports Car Club, and the GT350H made unofficial guest appearances at almost every drag strip in America.

The Mustang facelift in 1967 made it a much bigger car, so the Shelby version had to become a luxury GT with expensive options like air conditioning. In order to retain their performance profile Shelby cars had their own distinctive fiberglass front end to save weight, but even that was not enough. In 1967 the Shelby grew a new engine and the 428ci GT500 became the perform-ance option. It had been called the GT500 because Shelby thought it was a good name; similar reasoning to that which had named the original car on the basis that the distance from the engine shop to the assembly line was 'about' 350 feet.

With air conditioning, power steering, automatic gearbox and so on, the new cars were far more civilized and generally accept-able than the basic GT350 had been, which may be one reason why sales were far better. The other reason was probably linked with performance.

It was rumored that the GT500 could destroy a set of rear tires in a single evening of street racing; these were the cars advertised as the 'Road Cars,' and both Ford and Shelby were pleased with the performance, ride and handling compromise and even braking – Total Performance in every sense.

Ford were committed to Total Performance as a sales tool, so in 1967 Cobra production ended because Dearborn wanted to concentrate on the GT cars since they were a major boost to

Mustang sales and the Cobra had no street equivalent. Shelby filled the gap left by the Cobra and in 1968 began production of some of the most desirable cars ever – the convertible GT350 and 500.

In 1968 the GT350 got the new 302 smallblock, and in 1969 the Mustang got another facelift which added more weight and forced Shelby to come up with more fiberglass as well as adding the new 351 Windsor engine. Midway through the year came the 500KR (King of the Road), featuring the 428 Cobra Jet engine, and it replaced the standard GT500 from then on.

Shelby faced tough competition for their products from Ford's own Mustangs, the Boss 302, the Boss 429 and the Mach 1. A Shelby Mustang was almost impossible to insure (Shelbys had a horrific accident rate directly attributable to the fact that they had more power than most people knew what to do with) and they were among the most accident-prone cars in the history of the auto industry.

In addition the Federal ban on horsepower advertising was imminent, and so Shelby asked Ford to release him from the Total Performance program. The remaining 601 of the 1969 Shelby Mustangs were given airdams, black hood stripes and 1970 serial numbers. They were the last of the 14,368 Mustangs Shelby built; the days of legend were ended, although the Cobra now survives in more replica variants than any automobile outside the VW Beetle.

Inset left: The 1968 GT350 had a standard 302 V8 which produced 250hp – or 350 supercharged.

Left: The GT500 – all 360hp of it.

SUPERBIRD

Possibly the most excessive vehicles of the entire 1960s phenomenon were the droop-snoot NASCAR specials from Dodge and Plymouth, and it is perhaps fitting that these few cars – less than 2300 of both types were built – should have been the ones which saw the era die.

Initially something of a stopgap, the first cars to bear the Barracuda name were heavily modified Valiants with a fastback body style featuring, as Plymouth went to great lengths to point out, the largest rear window glass ever fitted to an automobile – 14.4 square feet. Plymouth had them in production only months after the launch of the Mustang.

The Dodge answer came in the Dart series, the neatest of what

Dodge eventually called the 'Scat Pack,' and its development parallelled that of the Barracuda to a large extent. Plymouth had offered a performance option ever since the 1956 Fury with its 426 engine, and these techniques were by no means new to the company. In fact the engineering was no problem whatsoever, and later, as the musclecar era developed, Plymouth mastered the requisite marketing techniques just as quickly.

While Barracuda was Plymouth's Mustang competitor it was competing in other performance areas too, where it was up against Pontiac and its own Dodge stablemates. In late 1963 it threw its 'orange monster' into this fight. This was no car, but the amazing 426-111 Super Stock hemi engine, the power behind their highly successful drag-racing effort which produced 26 track records in one season. With aluminum pistons and a high-lift cam it produced a highly respectable 425hp and secured endless titles for Dodge, including the 1962 NHRA championship. On every dragstrip across America the big motor was the supreme killer of the season. It was the outright wonder of NASCAR, where Dodge and Plymouth campaigned extensively, and secured a 1-2-3 victory at Daytona in 1964.

Above left: The 'orange monster' – the 426 street hemi – shared the honors with the slightly tamer 440 six-pack.

Above: The droop snoot and rear wing were genuine aerodynamic aids.

Left: As it appeared for NASCAR racing in just one year. The nosecone and wing were worth about 500 yards per lap.

It was only a year before the first street hemi became available; the Belvedere was a five-seat sedan which delivered a whopping 425hp. The Dodge version was the Coronet, which was possibly one of the better vehicles of the whole musclecar era.

The Dart GTS was the next episode in the story. With the 340-inch engine replaced by the huge 375hp 440 it had a top speed in excess of 120mph, saw off 100mph in 15 seconds and managed standing quarters in 14 seconds. The 426 hemi gave it an extra 55hp, but it also added a weight penalty of some 150lbs, giving it a handling disadvantage and making it a race-only option. With the Dart GTS came advanced versions of the rest of the Dodge Scat Pack, as Dodge adopted its Bumble Bee rear deck striping, and included one model designated Super Bee.

The year 1970 saw the advent of the new Dodge contender in the ponycar stakes – the all-new Challenger. This was lower and shorter than any other Dodge, having a small 110-inch wheelbase. It was also, with the possible exception of the fastback Charger, the best-looking member of the Scat Pack yet, with sleek 2-door sedan styling, and was years ahead of its time. Initially only the Challenger and Challenger R/T were available, with a slant-six standard and a 318 V8 optional in Challenger, against 383 as standard in the R/T. Options for the R/T included everything which was available, right up to the 440 six-pack and on to the 426 hemi. Plymouth development went with another part of the Belvedere lineup, the Satellite, and with the choice of 318, 383 or

426 wedge and the fabled 426 hemi engine this was a ready-to-race NASCAR winner straight off the showroom floor, and Richard Petty proved it winning the NASCAR Championship in 1967. The serious racer could, by ticking the right option boxes, produce a car from the showroom which was already up to track specification, and many did.

In 1968 the hemi became an exclusive option on the new GTX. This was the year in which a 1960s performance legend made its debut. The Belvedere had become first the Belvedere GTX, then the GTX and finally the GTX Road Runner, soon to be simply Roadrunner. Available as a hardtop or a coupe in its first year, it carried dummy hood scoops, special wheels, Road Runner nameplates and a cartoon bird decal on the sides and rear. It also had two engine options, and under the hood was either the 383 engine with manifolds and heads from the 440 or the genuine performance article – the 426 hemi.

The hemi had been available in a streetcar already, but it was in the Road Runner that it made the biggest impression; car and engine were well matched. *Motor Trend* voted it their Car of the Year in 1968, describing it as 'the simplest, starkest, most brazenly pure, non-compromising super car in history.' This description they applied to the 383, with its 440 heads and intake manifold. While not everybody could agree with *Motor Trend's* uncompromising attitude, there can be no doubt that the Road Runner was a special kind of car.

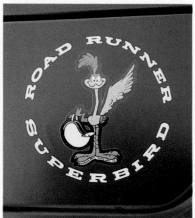

Left: The Road Runner name was drawn from a cartoon series.

Above right: The most common viewpoint.

Right and below: Along with the decals, buyers were also treated to a special two-tone 'beep-beep' horn based on the TV cartoon.

The starting point was the (very) basic Belvedere body, completely lacking in convenience and luxury features. The Road Runner emphasis was simply on performance. This was not a car which Plymouth were curbing within price constraints. The Road Runner was given everything it needed and the price was allowed to settle wherever it might. An unusual and rather brave technique, especially for the period, it paid off handsomely, since the basic 383 was only a few hundred dollars over the current market average, although a few hundred dollars could buy quite a lot in the mid-1960s.

For these few hundred dollars came the 383, a handling package with sway bar, heavy-duty shocks, huge torsion bar and heavy rear leaf springs. Although *Motor Trend* clearly admired it, even they were forced to concede that all that extra springing still could not compensate for the weight of the engine; the eternal compromise between ride and handling had as usual come down in favor of a comfortable ride. Even wide tires could not completely disguise the fact that the 383 could hurl the 3660lbs of Road Runner around at frightening speed.

By 1969 dummy hood scoops had become a real cold-air induction system called Air Grabber on the GTX and Coyote Duster in the Road Runner, but this was mere preparation for the genuine article which was shortly to follow.

The year 1970 saw what was the last fling for Mopar and the musclecar itself when Plymouth unveiled their final entry into the Rapid Transit System. Designed for the 200mph NASCAR speedways, the Superbird was the ultimate Road Runner. Dual quad carbs gave the 426 hemi 425hp, and the Superbird had an aerodynamically-shaped droop-snoot concealing pop-up headlamps and a huge rear wing. Offered for one year only, a mere 1920 were built. The Superbird was a follow-up to the 1969 Dodge Daytona Charger, which had been built especially for the Daytona meeting, and it was this which lay behind the pointed nosecone and rear stabilizer. The Daytona Charger's aerodynamics were about 20 percent more efficient than the previous year's Charger. This meant that it was 500 yards better off each lap – an advantage well worth having. Some 505 of these cars were built – just the right number to homologate as a NASCAR production car, and running with its Plymouth cousin, the Daytona and Superbird dominated the 1970 NASCAR season, winning 38 out of 48 races.

INDEX

*Page numbers in italics refer to
illustrations*

AC Company 116
American Graffiti film 71
Ardun hemihead conversion 41
Ash, David 110
Auburn cars 30, 31, 33, 34, 38, 47
  1929 120 Speedster 31, *32*, 33
  1935 Speedster *33*
  1970 120 Speedster 33
Auburn company 15, 30-31, 46, 47
Auburn-Cord-Duesenberg 33, 34, 36, 38,
  47, 86
  see also Auburn, Cord, Dusenberg
Autorama car show 62

Baker, 'Cannonball' 14
Bard, Ralph 30
Barnato, 'Babe' 15
Barr, Harry 66
Barrow, Clyde 41
Beaver engines 20
Bentley, W O 14
Bentley cars 12, 14-15
Bourke, Robert 92
Breech, Ernest 77
Breedlove, Craig 118
Brewster (Rolls-Royce America) 36
Briggs coachwork 53
Buehrig, Gordon 31, 47
Bugatti cars 20
Buick cars 30, 70, 73
  Y-Job *48-9*

Cadillac, Antoine 84
Cadillac cars 26, 70, 84
  1930s V16 Sedan de Ville 84, 86
  Cyclone 86, 88
  Eldorado *84-9*, 86, 88
    Biarritz *85*, 86, 88
    Brougham 86, 88
    Fleetwood *86-7*
    Seville 86, 88
  La Salle 27
Cadillac company 27, 51, 84
Cadillac engines
  1914 V8 84
  1931 454 V16 86
  1954 V8 57, 88
Camaro *see* chevrolet
Car and Driver 103
Car assembly 12, 20

Carrozzeria Padana 15
Central Manufacturing Company 31
Chevrolet cars 66, 70-71, 88, 90
  1955-7 series 66, 70, 71
    Bel Air *66-71*, 70
  Biscayne 71
  Camaro 64, 104, 109, 113, 115
    Iroc-Z 104
    Z-28 96, 104, *105-9*, 109
  Corvette 20, 57, *62-5*, 81, 95, 110, 116
    description and development 62,
      64-5, 70, 78
  Fiero 64
  Firebird 64, 113, 115
  Impala 71
  Make Shark (Sting Ray) 65
  Nomad Station Wagon 70
Chevrolet company 56, 92, 104
  Division of General Motors 104
Chevrolet engines
  229 V6 64
  302 V8 104, 109
  350 Vfl 104, 109
  smallblock V8 41, 62, 64, 66, 70, 96
  stovebolt six 62
Christie, Walter 46
Chrysler cars 48
  Airflow 48
Chrysler company 15
  Chrysler engine 48
  331 smallblock hemi 96
coast-to-coast record 14, 23
Cobra see Shelby Cobra
Cole, Ed 62, 66
Colt, Samuel 84
Cord, Erret Lobban 30, 31, 33, 34, 36, 38,
  45-7
Cord cars 34
  1929-31 L-29 *44*, 46
  1935 810 Series 47
    'Coffin nose' Westchester Sedan *45, 47*
  1936 812 *46*
  1937 Convertible *46*
Corvette *see* Chevrolet
Crusoe, Lewis 81
Curtiss-Wright company 28, 92

Darrin, Howard 'Dutch' 27, 56, 57
  Kaiser-Darrin car 56-7, *56-7*
Dayton Electric Laboratories (General
    Motors Delco Division) 84
Daytona race meetings 71, 96, 118, 122, 125
Delling, Erik 20
De Lorean, John Z 65, 96, 101
de Palma, Ralph 21
Depression, The 26, 33, 38, 41, 47, 84
Derham coachwork *34*, 38
Detroit Automobile Manufacturing
    Company 7, 84
Dewar Trophy 84, 86
Dietrich coachwork *23*, 26
Dodge brothers 12
Dodge cars 72, 122, 124
  Challenger 124

Charger, Daytona Charger 124, 125
  Coronet 122
  Dart Series 122
    GTS 122, 124
    Scat Pack series 122, 124
drag racing 41, 96, 118, 120, 122
Duesenberg brothers, Fred and August
  34, 36, 38
Duesenberg cars 34, 38, 47
  1920 Model A 34
  1929 Model J Roadster 34, *35*, 36, 38
  Le baron Phaeton *36*
  1932 Model SJ *34*, 38
  1933 Speedster *36*
  1935 Speedster *37*
  1966 model 15
Duesenberg company 15, 30, 34, 38, 46
Duntov, Zora Arkus 41, 62, 64, 65
Durant, William 46, 84

Earl, Harley 56, 70, 86
Eckert brothers 30
Edsel *see* Ford cars
Edward VIII 48
Eldorado *see* Cadillac
Estes, Peter 96, 101
Eugene, Prince, of Belgium 26
Exner, Virgil 15, 70, 92

Ferrari, Enzo 78
Ferrari cars 78, 103, 118
  GTO 103
  Superamerica 70
Fetch, Tom 23
Fiberglass introduced 56
Fleetwood coachwork 86, *86*
Foote, Cone and Belding 76
Ford, Benson 53
Ford, Edsel 51, 53, 55, 72, 77, 84
Ford, Henry 7-8, 12, 40, 41, 51, 53, 55, 72, 84
  and Henry Leland 8, 51, 55, 84
  mass production introduced by 7, 84
Ford, Henry II 53, 55, 73, 77
Ford cars 70, 90
  early models A, B, C, N 8
  'Arrow,' '999' 40
  Model T *3*, 7-8, *8*, 10, 20, 40, 45, 53
    description 10, 40
    1909-15 models *3, 8, 9*
    1921-27 models *10, 11*
  Model A 40
  Model B 40, 41, 66
    Roadster *40, 42-3*
  Model 18 (Model 40) *40*, 41
  Model C 8
  Edsel 66, 72, *72-4*, 77, *77*
    Citation 73, *74*, 76
    Corsair 73, 76, 77
    Pacer 73, 76
    Ranger 73, *73*, 76, 77, *77*
  Fairlane 8, 70, 73, 77, 118
  Falcon 8, 118
  Frontenac Fords 26, 40

Galaxie 8, 118
GT 118, 120
  GT40 15, 120
Mustang 82, 104, 109, 110, *111-15*, 113,
    115, 116, 120, 122
  description 110, 113, 115
  notchback hardtop coupe 113
  Shelby and 64, *116, 119*, 120, 121
  Boss Mustang 115, 121
  Mach I *112*, 115, 121
  Sportsroof coupe *114-15*
Thunderbird 64, 78, *78-83*, 81-2, 95, 110,
    115
  description 81
see also Lincoln, Mercury, Shelby
    Cobra
Ford engines 40-41, *77*, 110, 113, 115, 116
  flathead V8 40, 41, *60*, 62, 66, 78
  L-head V12 53, 55
  Y-block V8 41, 81, 82
  smallblock V8 73, 76, 116
  410 bigblock 76
  430 bigblock 82
  427 33, 118, 120
Ford Motor Company 8, 40, 56, 72, 73, 77,
    81, 92, 95, 118
  Total Performance Policy 110, 116, 120,
    121
Frazer, Joseph 56
French Grand Prix 34
front-wheel drive introduced 46

General Motors Corporation 20, 46, 48, 56,
    62, 64, 66, 72, 81, 84, 86, 95, 96, 116
  Divisions
    Art and Design 104
    Buick *see* Buick cars
    Cadillac *see* Cadillac cars, company
    Delco Division 84
    Pontiac *see* Pontiac cars
    Styling 48
  'no racing' edict 96
Getty, Paul 88
Glass Reinforced Plastic (GRP) introduced
    56
Gregorie, Bob 53
GT *see* Ford, Shelby Cobra
GTO *see* Pontiac cars

Halderman, Gayle 110
Hare, Emlen 21
hemispherical cylinder head engine 96,
    122, 124
Henry Ford Manufacturing Company 8, 51,
    84
Hershey, Frank 81
Hertz Company, Sports Car Club 120
Hoffman, Paul 90
Hupmobile car 90
Hurley, Roy 28

Iacocca, Lee 82, 110, 116

Indianapolis race meetings 12, 96

Jaguar cars 57
  XK Series 78
Jenkins, 'Mormon Meteor' Ab 33

Kaiser, Henry J 56
Kaiser-Darrin car 56-7, *56-7*
Kaiser-Frazer car 56-7
Kaufmann, Bud 82
Kettering, 'Boss' 84
Knudsen, 'Big Bill' 96
Knudsen, Semon 'Bunkie' 96
Krause, Billy 116
Kuser family 20

La Salle *see* Cadillac cars
Le Baron, coachbuilder 27, *29, 36*, 38
Lehman brothers 56
Leland, Henry M 8, 12, 51, 55, 72, 84, 86
  and Henry Ford 8, 51, 55, 84
Leland-Faulconer engines 12
Le Mans race meetings 12, 14-15, 62, 118,
    120
Lexington Motor Company 31
Limousine Body Company 31
Lincoln cars 26, 33, 51, 88
  1929 Dual Cowl Phaeton *50-51*
  1937, 1940 V12 Zephyr *52*, 53-4
  1942 Continental *52*, 53-4, *54-5*, 55, 72, 82
Lincoln company 51, 55, 84
Lincoln-Mercury Division of Ford 51, 53,
    55, 73, 84
Lockhart, Frank 14
Loewy, Raymond 90, 92, 95
Lycoming company 30, 33, 34, 46
Lycoming engines 30, 33, 34, 36, 38, 47
Lyons, William 78

McDonald, Stewart 30
MacKichan, Clare 70
McLellan, Dave 65
McRae, Duncan 95
mass production 7, 84
Mercer cars 12, 14, 19-20
  1909 Model 30-C Speedster 20
  1913 Model 35-J *18*
    L-head engine 20, 21
  Raceabout 12, 20-21
    1912 model *18*
    1921-2 model *20-21*
Mercer company 21
Mercury (Lincoln) cars 27, *58-9*, 73, 76
  Cougar 115
  Series 09A
MG cars 57, 78
Miller, Harry 31, 46
Mitchell, Bill 65, 104
Monkees pop group 103
Moon, Dean 116
Moon Motor Car Company 30, 45-6

Moore, Marianne 76, 77
Motor Trend 124, 125
Motorama shows 48
Murphy coachwork *35*, 38
musclecars 96, *97*, 101, *102*, 103, *107, 113*,
    115, 122, 125
Muscovics, Frederic 14
Mustang *see* Ford cars, Shelby Cobra

Nance, Jim 23, 28
NASCAR race meetings 71, 96, 115, 122,
    124, 125
Nesmith, Mike 103
Nuffield, Lord 78

Oldfield, Barney 21
Olds, Ransom E 84
Oldsmobile cars 70
Oros, Joe 110

Packard, James 23
Packard, Samuel 26
Packard cars 23, 26, 27, 28, 36, 84
  Model F (1903) 23
  K Type Gray Wolf (1904) 26
  Thirty Thirty Roadster (1910) 26
  Twin Six 26
  633 Roadster (1929) *23*
  734 Speedster (1929) 26, *27*
  745 Sports Phaeton *24-5*
  1105 Coupe Roadster (1933) *27*
  V12 (1932-4) *23, 27*
  V12 Coupe (1937) *28*
  8-cylinder One Twenty 26
  Darrin Victoria 27
  Straight Six One-Ten 26
  eight-seater *29*
  1608 Rollston DC Phaeton *29*
  Caribbean Convertible *28*
Packard company 23, 26, 27-8, 84, 92
Palmer, Jerry 65
Petty, Richard 124
Piggins, Vincent 109
Pininfarina company 88
Plymouth cars 70, 90, 122, 124
  Barracuda 122
  Belvedere 122, 124
    GTX Roadrunner 124, *124-5*, 125
    Superbird 125
  Fury 122
  426 Super Stock hemi 122, *123*, 124, 125
Plymouth 383 engine 124-5
Pontiac cars 72
  Grand Prix 15
  GTO 96, *97-102*, 101, 103
  Tempest 96, 97, *100-101*, 101, *102*
Pontiac company 65, 96, 101, 103
Pontiac V8 engine 15, 96, 101
Porsche, Ferdinand 78
Porsche cars 57, 62, 78
Porter, Finlay Robertson 20, 21
Poyer, Bill 81